Grammar Dimensions
Book One
Form, Meaning, and Use

Teacher's Manual

Victoria Badalamenti

LaGuardia Community College

Carolyn Henner-Stanchina

Queens College

Heinle & Heinle Publishers
A Division of Wadsworth, Inc.
Boston, Massachusetts 02116 U.S.A

Copyright © 1993 by Heinle & Heinle Publishers

All rights reserved. No part of this publication may be reproduced or transmitted in any form or by any means, electronic, or mechanical, including photocopy, recording, or any information storage or retrieval system, without permission in writing from the publisher.

ISBN 0-8384-4127-0

10 9 8 7 6 5 4 3 2

Table of Contents

	Introduction to Teacher's Manual — *Grammar Dimensions: Form, Meaning, and Use*	v
	Teaching a Sample Unit **Unit 10: *There + Be***	viii
Unit 1	• The Verb *Be* **Affirmative Statements; Subject Pronouns**	1
Unit 2	• The Verb *Be* **Yes/No Questions; *Be* + Adjective; Negative Statements**	5
Unit 3	• The Verb *Be* **Wh-Questions**	9
Unit 4	• Noun Phrases **Count and Non-Count Nouns**	12
Unit 5	• The Verb *Have* **Affirmative/Negative; Questions and Short Answers; *Some/Any***	17
Unit 6	• Possessives **Nouns, Adjectives, and Pronouns; Questions with *Whose*; *A/An* versus *The***	23
Unit 7	• Demonstratives **Pronouns and Adjectives**	29
Unit 8	• *Be* + Prepositional Phrase; *Where* Questions	33
Unit 9	• Intensifiers ***Be* + Adjective + Noun**	37
Unit 10	• *There + Be*	40

Unit 11 •	Simple Present Tense **Affirmative and Negative Statements; Time Expressions; *In/On/At*; *Make* and *Do***	41
Unit 12 •	Simple Present Tense **Questions; Adverbs of Frequency**	48
Unit 13 •	Imperatives	54
Unit 14 •	Prepositions of Direction	58
Unit 15 •	Direct Objects and Object Pronouns	61
Unit 16 •	*Can* versus *Know How To; And/But*	64
Unit 17 •	Adverbs of Manner	68
Unit 18 •	Present Progressive Tense	71
Unit 19 •	Past Tense of *Be*	77
Unit 20 •	Past Tense	83
Unit 21 •	Indirect Objects with *To*	91
Unit 22 •	Reflexive and Reciprocal Pronouns	95
Unit 23 •	Future Time ***Will* and *Be Going To***	99
Unit 24 •	Quantifiers	104
Unit 25 •	Adjective Phrases	108
Unit 26 •	Phrasal Verbs	112
Unit 27 •	Comparison with Adjectives	116
Unit 28 •	Comparison with Adverbs	121
Unit 29 •	Superlatives	124
Unit 30 •	Factual Conditionals	127

Introduction to Teacher's Manual — *Grammar Dimensions: Form, Meaning, and Use*

Theoretical Assumptions

Grammar Dimensions rests on a number of assumptions about language and the teaching/learning process. Some of the assumptions are supported by empirical findings; others have been arrived at experientially. In order for the series to be used to best advantage, it is important that the assumptions be made explicit. There are ten:

1. Teachers should be seeking ways of integrating a focus on form or grammar with one on communicative use, rather than on perpetuating the misguided assumption that one must choose between methods that favor one or the other.

2. Grammar does not merely refer to structures or forms. All grammar structures reflect the three dimensions of **form, meaning,** and **use.** For example, the English present progressive consists of some present tense **form** of the verb BE and the present participle, the morpheme *-ing*. The **meaning** the *-ing* ascribes to a verb is that the action/event is in process and, therefore, incomplete. Thus, one of the **uses** of the present progressive is to signal a temporary, as opposed to an enduring, state of affairs (cf. *Peter is living with his parents; Peter lives with his parents*). All three dimensions must be mastered if a student is to be able to use grammar structures **accurately, meaningfully,** and **appropriately.**

3. One of the questions teachers must ask themselves is, "What can I give my students that they can't easily get on their own?" One answer to this question is that I can help draw their attention systematically to the features of the language. They might eventually notice these features on their own, but my calling attention to them will accelerate the process whereby the input to which my students are exposed becomes intake for their acquisition process. Focusing student attention on some aspect of each one of these three dimensions at a time will help my students to develop their own inner criteria for correctness and aid them in the process of self-monitoring.

4. Classroom time is limited. Teachers should not waste time "teaching" students what they already know. Teachers can use student performance as a basis for assessing what it is they need to and are ready to learn.

5. All three dimensions of grammar do not present an equally difficult learning challenge for all learners. Some structures present more of a structural challenge; for others, the long-term challenge is to learn what the structures mean or when to use them. The type and degree of challenge vary according to the inherent complexity of the structure itself and the particular language background and level of English proficiency of the learner. Teachers must continuously ask themselves, "What is the learning challenge of the point I am teaching for this particular group of learners?" They must then devise activities that are likely to afford learning opportunities commensurate with the degree, and appropriate to the type, of challenge.

6. It is likely that there is a sequence of development with regard to learning a language such that learners will not acquire a certain aspect of the target language until they are ready to do so. Teaching does not cause learning. Teachers should not, therefore, expect students to perform perfectly something that has already been introduced. They should, instead, return to the teaching point from time to time, reviewing and expanding upon it.

7. Although grammar is often thought of as an area of language, as opposed to a skill like reading, writing, speaking, or listening, it is in fact a skill. We do not want students simply to know about the language or to be able to recite a rule; we want students to be able to use the grammar. Perhaps we should think of what we do as teaching the skill of "grammaring." As with any skill, mastery takes practice.

8. Learning is enhanced when students are engaged in a variety of purposeful, personally meaningful, and enjoyable activities.

9. Students should be led to make generalizations of the highest level possible. For example, rather than learning the present progressive, the past progressive, and the future progressive as individual phenomena, they should learn the general meaning of the *-ing* morpheme as it applies to all three.

10. The acquisition process is not a linear one. Students do not master one structure before going on to tackle another. Moreover, when new structures are introduced, students often backslide with regard to some other aspect of grammar that presumably had already been learned. This may be evidence that the learners' understanding of how English works is being reconfigured. Thus, a temporary lapse in students' performance may actually be evidence of progress.

Distinctive Features of the Series

There are a number of ways these theoretical assumptions about language and the teaching/learning process contribute to the distinctive features of the series.

1. Each unit begins with a communicative **Task.** While engaging in the task, students are using language for communicative or pragmatic purposes. The tasks themselves, however, have been constructed to include instances of the target structure. In this way learners first encounter the target grammar structure in a meaningful context. Thus, the use of communicative tasks provides one way in which grammar and communication can be integrated.

    Another benefit of using tasks is that student performance on the task can be diagnosed by the teacher to determine learning needs. Students may demonstrate that they have already learned what they need to know about a target structure, in which case the unit can be skipped entirely; or it may be possible for the teacher to pinpoint precisely where the students need to work. In this way, teachers can tailor their courses to best meet learner needs and thus contribute to the effective use of limited class time.

2. Relevant facts about the **form, meaning,** and **use** of the target structure are presented in **Focus Boxes** following the task. Student attention can be specifically directed to certain of these focus boxes depending upon the learning challenge for the particular audience of students or the relative importance of the linguistic facts presented. Alternatively, a teacher might choose to work systematically through all the focus boxes in a given unit. Then, too, it is possible for a teacher to decide to work on a portion of a unit and then set it aside to go on to another target structure. Later, the teacher can return to the original unit in a way that allows for review and expansion.

3. Following each focus box is at least one **Exercise** related to the content of the box. The exercises are varied, but every attempt has been made to make them purposeful (e.g., there is no meaningless repetition), personally meaningful (i.e., students are frequently asked to register some opinion or to explain why they chose the answer they did), and enjoyable (thematically coherent and often with "human interest" foci). Besides the exercises in the text, additional exercises can be found in a supplementary workbook which will help give students further practice with "grammaring."

4. At the end of each of the units is a series of **Activities** which help students realize the communicative value of the grammar they are learning. As a complement to the communicative task that opened the unit, grammar and communication are again practiced in tandem. Teachers can use student performance on these activities to assess what students have learned and where they still need to work. Teachers should not, however, expect perfect performance at this point.

5. Additional features of the series which address the remaining assumptions are:
   - a **discourse focus** which enables students to generalize at the highest level of language and which helps them learn how to use structures appropriately in context;
   - **free-standing** units which teachers can choose to skip entirely or to sequence in a particular order based upon the unique composition of their class; and
   - a **comprehensive** scope of grammatical structures that spans level of difficulty from beginning to highly advanced, thus meeting the learning needs of learners at all levels of English proficiency.

Diane Larsen-Freeman

Teaching a Sample Unit
Unit 10: *There + Be*

Introduction

The general introduction to the series explains the assumptions about the teaching/learning process on which this book is based, and the distinctive focus on the **form, meaning,** and **use** of each target structure.

In this section, we underline in general terms the implications of adopting this task-based communicative approach for beginning level students. Recent expanded notions of "communicative competence" involve four areas of knowledge and skills:

- linguistic competence
- sociolinguistic competence
- discourse competence
- strategic competence

Linguistic competence is probably the most familiar of these notions. However, because the underlying assumption here is that linguistic competence is achieved through meaningful repetition rather than through decontextualized drills, the grammar structures are presented through Tasks, and the Exercises are designed to be as communicative as possible.

TASKS

The Tasks require learners to interact with each other, to think, answer questions, or use their own background knowledge in order to make decisions or solve problems of some sort. Students can complete the Tasks in pairs, in small groups, or even individually. We do recommend bringing the whole class back together to discuss the various solutions, ideas, or answers that each group has come up with. Students enjoy this, and it will provide you with interesting, useful information about the students and their ability to use the language.

The Tasks are designed either to expose learners to the target structure, or to motivate the use of that structure. Remember that students are not expected to know or be able to produce the target structure correctly in the Task. Some of the target structures are presented deductively; others in a more inductive way, allowing you to elicit observations about **form, meaning,** and **use** from your students before providing them with the rules. You may want to focus on the language generated by the students, write their hypotheses on the board, examine them, and then introduce the target structure once the need for the structure has become clear.

FOCUS BOXES

Similarly, how you use the Focus Boxes will depend on the approach you adopt in each unit. In a deductive approach, you may want to begin with the Focus Box and then have your students apply the rule by doing the Exercises. In a more inductive approach, you might want to have students examine and figure out the structure first, then do the Exercises, then refer to the Focus Box at the end to confirm and solidify the rules. Throughout this manual, we will try to provide suggestions on varying the use of the Tasks and Focus Boxes.

VOCABULARY

In creating meaningful, engaging contexts that respect the adults' experience and knowledge base, it is necessary to introduce a good deal of new vocabulary, even to students at low proficiency levels. We have tried to incorporate an implicit focus on vocabulary in the first phase of some of the Tasks. However, you may decide that you need to pre-teach this vocabulary explicitly, to help learners match their existing conceptual knowledge to the new words, in those cases where you feel that these new words would be particularly challenging to your students. For example, in Unit 5 ("The Verb *Have*"), it would probably be advisable to discuss the Inuit photos first, elaborating the vocabulary needed to complete the Task. However, in Unit 6 ("Possessives"), since learners can match the items to their owners without knowing the vocabulary, you might not find it necessary to pre-teach the vocabulary. Your decisions will depend on a variety of factors: how much you want to challenge the students, how inductive an approach you opt for, how much ambiguity your students can tolerate, how much time you have, how much experience you have using this book, etc.

EXERCISES

You will note the recurring Exercise types. *Test Your Knowledge* Exercises call upon the learners' background knowledge or experience and encourage them to think. *Information Gap* and *Find Someone Who* Exercises create a need and an environment conducive to real communication. This gives more meaning to the repetition of the structures. *Error Correction* Exercises are based on the confusions and errors typically observed in the performance of students at this level. The purpose of these Exercises is to raise the students' level of awareness and to develop in them the ability to recognize their own errors and monitor their own performance. When it becomes obvious to you that students are still confused about certain structures, you may want to refer them back to the appropriate Focus Boxes.

There are other Exercises that encourage learners to go beyond what is explicitly stated and use the given context to make predictions and inferences. Because these types of Exercises are less familiar to students, they will probably need more help and guidance in doing them. For example, in Unit 5, Exercise 4, learners are required to ask and answer questions based on their own inferences. The answers are not in the text. By having them discuss these questions in groups and verbalize how they came to their respective conclusions, you will be inviting them to think, as well as to repeat the structures in a natural situation.

How you go about checking these Exercises is up to you. You can have students:

- take turns answering the questions with the whole class together;
- write their answers on the board and check them all together;
- write their answers on large sheets of newsprint that are hung up around the room. Then have students circulate to check their own papers against these;
- check their work in pairs or groups;
- check their work against an answer sheet you have provided.

Although we have provided directions for each Exercise, please consider these as suggestions. The nature of your class, their needs and objectives, their response to this material, their preferences for working alone or cooperatively, and your own beliefs about language learning will all affect the way you use this book. Do not hesitate to change an oral Exercise into a written one, to skip Exercises, to change the steps in an Exercise, to change the class configuration, etc.

Sociolinguistic competence includes knowledge of speech acts as well as the ability to vary language appropriately according to the person(s) one is addressing. For example, Unit 13 deals with the functions and appropriate uses of imperatives. Other Use Focus Boxes dealing with speech acts can be found in:

- Unit 1   (Introducing)
- Unit 3   (Talking about the Time/the Weather)
- Unit 4   (Asking about Prices)
- Unit 5   (Making Polite Requests/Describing People)
- Units 7 and 9   (Asking for Information)
- Unit 11   (Talking about Habits, Routines/Making Generalizations)
- Unit 14   (Giving Directions)
- Unit 23   (Expressing Intentions or Prior Plans)
- Unit 27   (Using Negative Equatives for Politeness)

Discourse competence reflects an awareness of how grammar is used to focus information and achieve cohesion. In this book, some of the **Use** Focus Boxes attempt to develop greater awareness of the importance of context in making grammatical choices; particularly of the role of word order in the presentation of "given" and "new" information in English. This attention to discourse competence has led us to explain certain structures in ways that may seem unusual or surprising to you. For example, in Unit 10, Focus Box 1 seeks to explain the position of new information after the verb *be*, with *there* acting as a subject filler. This is why a grammatically correct sentence ("A cat is under the bed") may still not be the appropriate sentence to use when showing the existence or location of something that represents new information ("There's a cat under the bed.") This will be further explained in the Sample Unit. You will find other instances of the "given–new contract" in Units 21 and 30. Unit 6 ("Possessives") deals with the difference between the indefinite and the definite articles. Exercises 12 and 13 provide contexts in which learners must apply principles of discourse — presupposition and raising to consciousness — to the selection of articles. Articles can potentially cause problems for ESL learners throughout the course of their learning. We hope this approach will allow them entry into the article system at an early stage.

Strategic competence generally refers to a set of communication strategies that learners employ in order to compensate for their lack of linguistic knowledge, to repair breakdowns in communication, and to maintain the interaction while learning more about how English works. Units 3, 13, and 16 attempt to teach these communication strategies. In addition, Unit 12 takes a broader view of strategic competence, introducing learner strategies and the learning process itself. We have deliberately invited learners to reflect on and discuss their own strategies, hoping that they will become better, more autonomous learners as a result of this awareness-raising.

We suggest that you have students keep learning journals throughout the course. They should be encouraged to write about all aspects of their learning experience — how they feel about learning and using English, what they do to understand and produce language, how they organize their learning, how they remember what they learn, and how they compensate for what they don't know.

We also urge you to have students keep grammar journals in which they would record all feedback on the accuracy and appropriateness of their own output. Students must be shown how to organize a grammar journal, where each structure could be listed on a separate page. Students would enter their own errors on these pages along with the corrections. In this way, students would have a clear profile of their error types and grammar problems by the end of the course.

In summary, we hope that in seeking to develop the four levels of communicative competence, this book will provide a richer, more authentic context for learning; a context that proves more enjoyable to you and your students.

Teaching Unit 10: *There + Be*

The first focus of the Unit is the discourse difference between two sentences that are both grammatically correct. In such a case, how can students know which sentence to select? The discourse rule, or "given-new contract," means that to show the existence or location of new information, we use *there* in the subject position in front of the verb *be*, followed by a noun phrase headed by an indefinite article. *There* serves as a dummy subject that holds the subject position open and allows the new information to be postponed. The verb *be* agrees with the noun phrase that follows it. Native speakers of English describing the picture in the Task would automatically choose "There's a cat under the bed," rather than "A cat is under the bed." Exercise 1 requires students to make this discourse choice.

We believe it is helpful to explain that *there* is in the subject position to allow for the postponement of new information. This may seem too difficult or complex to teach at this level. However, this explanation reinforces the English subject–verb word order and facilitates understanding of question formation. "Is there a cat under the bed" follows more logically when we know that *there* is in the subject position. This explanation also respects the discourse rule governing the positioning of new information and is less confusing than saying that the noun phrase is really the subject of the sentence but comes after the verb in both statements and questions. This rule also governs our choices of other structures, some of which appear in this book. For example, in Unit 21 we have introduced the same rule to aid students in deciding whether to place an indirect object pronoun before a direct object pronoun, or vice versa. The rule appears again in Unit 30 on the ordering of clauses in Factual Conditionals.

The presentation of the structure in this Unit is more inductive than in most of the other Units in this book. In the Task, students study the picture and decide whose apartment this is. At this point, students are not expected to produce the structure; nor are they even exposed to the structure. However, the Task sets up the need to use the structure *There + Be,* which students are required to produce in Exercise 2.

As is true for all the Tasks in this book, the Task may be used for diagnostic purposes. If you feel your class already has knowledge of this structure, you may want to ask students to produce sentences describing what they see in the Task. Have students write their sentences on the board. This will give you an opportunity to analyze their hypotheses, point out the errors, and come back to Focus Boxes 1 and 2 to explain why their sentences are incorrect.

However, even if your class is seeing this structure for the first time, you can still ask them to form sentences right after the Task or after Focus Box 1. You might say, "From the Task, we know that the woman in this apartment has a cat. What sentence can we write to express this?" Have them write their hypotheses on the board. In all probability, they will not produce the target structure. Then discuss Focus Boxes 1 and 2, and come back to their hypotheses in order to emphasize the special nature of the structure *There + Be*.

TASK

1. The person is a woman.
2. She doesn't have a baby.
3. She has a pet.
4. She's athletic.
5. She is a coffee drinker.
6. She's well-educated.
7. She is not a smoker. / She isn't a smoker.
8. She's middle-class.
9. She's a music lover.
10. She is not on a diet. / She's not on a diet. / She isn't on a diet.

EXERCISE 1

1. a.   2. b.   3. b.

EXERCISE 2

You'll notice that we have not included *there* or the verb *be* in the cues. This is to see whether students can spontaneously generate sentences that are correct in both form and use. Have students write their sentences on the board so that you can examine any problems together: omission of *there*, use of *have* instead of *be*, errors involving singular/non-count or plural nouns, etc. Since *some/any* was introduced in Unit 5, you may want to recycle *some* here.

1. There's one bed in the apartment.
2. There's (some) women's clothing in the closet.
3. There are high-heeled shoes in the closet.
4. There's (some) women's jewelry in the box on the dresser.
5. There's a tennis racquet in the closet.
6. There are sneakers in the closet.
7. There's an exercise bicycle in the apartment.
8. There's a coffee pot on the stove.
9. There are (some) books on the shelf.
10. There's a computer on the desk.
11. There's an expensive rug on the floor.
12. There's a fur coat in the closet.
13. There are (some) records on the shelf.
14. There's (some) stereo equipment on the shelf.
15. There's a big cake on the counter.

EXERCISE 3

This exercise gives students a chance to use the structure for a purpose — to describe a scene that others must draw. Check their drawings by putting them up around the room, or by circulating them to see which do or do not correspond to the description. Students will enjoy looking at each other's art work.

FOCUS 3

This Focus Box deals with negative statements with *There + Be*. We have introduced the structure

There is no
There's no } drinking water on the island because it occurs frequently. However, this structure is likely to lead to

incorrect utterances such as "There no is drinking water on the island." Students may initially be confused about the use of *no* for negation in front of a noun phrase, as opposed to the use of *no* for negation on the verb (*is + not*). Monitor their performance closely to avoid this confusion.

EXERCISE 4

This exercise includes items that are found in the apartment as well as items not found there so that it is not merely a repetition drill.

1. There's no television set in the apartment./
   There isn't any television set in the apartment.
2. There's a rug in the apartment.
3. There's no men's clothing in the apartment./
   There isn't any men's clothing in the apartment.
4. There's a computer in the apartment.
5. There are no ashtrays in the apartment./
   There aren't any ashtrays in the apartment.
6. There are no cigarettes in the apartment./
   There aren't any cigarettes in the apartment.

7. There are (some) books in the apartment.
8. There aren't any toys in the apartment./
   There are no toys in the apartment.
9. There's an exercise bicycle in the apartment.
10. There's no crib in the apartment./
    There isn't any crib in the apartment.
11. There's a coffee pot in the apartment.
12. There aren't any ties in the apartment./
    There are no ties in the apartment.

EXERCISE 5

This exercise is about a city named Utopia. Students must understand the concept of Utopia before they can do Exercises 5 and 6.

We have structured this exercise so that students must make affirmative and negative statements as indicated. You could make this exercise more challenging by eliminating the yes/no columns and allowing students to judge whether or not the city Utopia has the item in question. One possibility would be to write each item on an index card, have students pick a card, read the item aloud, and make an appropriate statement. You may want to add other elements to this list. You may also take this opportunity to discuss nuances in meaning when *some* or *any* is used.

In Utopia...
- There are no guns. / There aren't any guns.
- There's public transportation.
- There's no crime. / There isn't any crime.
- There are museums.
- There's no traffic. / There isn't any traffic.
- There are universities.
- There's no noise. / There isn't any noise.
- There are jobs.
- There are parks.
- There are no poor people. / There aren't any poor people.

EXERCISE 6

Ensure that students understand the meaning of *politician* and that they realize they must use the context of the exercise to determine whether the statements should be affirmative or negative. After they've completed the exercise, have them role-play the text. You might have them change this to an interview between a journalist and the Mayor of Utopia. They could write the questions and answer them based on this context.

(1) there are
(2) There are no / There aren't any
(3) There are
(4) There are
(5) There are
(6) There are no / There aren't any
(7) There is no (There's no) / There isn't any
(8) There are no / There aren't any
(9) There is no (There's no) / There isn't any
(10) There is no (There's no) / There isn't any
(11) There are
(12) There is (There's)
(13) There is (There's)
(14) There are
(15) There is (There's)

FOCUS 4

Again, it will be easier for students to understand question formation with *There + Be* once they know that *there* is in the subject position. Be sure that they do not omit *there* in the questions.

EXERCISE 7

This exercise uses common situations to elicit the structure.

1. Are there (any) messages for me?
2. Is there a doctor in the house?
3. Is there anything in here to eat, Mom?
4. Is there a post office near here?
5. Are there (any) tickets available for the 10:00 show?
6. Is there (any) room for me?
7. Are there (any) instructions in the box?
8. Is there (any) mail for me?
9. Are there (any) small sizes?
10. Are there (any) witnesses?

EXERCISE 8

This exercise requires students to use their own background knowledge to answer the questions. You may want to review the use of *any* during this exercise. Encourage students to ask each other more questions like these.

1. *Is there any rain in a desert?*
   No, there isn't.
2. *Are there twelve planets in our solar system?*
   No, there aren't. There are nine (Mercury, Venus, Earth, Mars, Jupiter, Saturn, Uranus, Neptune, Pluto).
3. *Are there two billion people in China?*
   No, there aren't. There are one billion people in China.
4. *Are there 52 states in the United States?*
   No, there aren't. There are 50 states.
5. *Are there any earthquakes in California?*
   Yes, there are.
6. *Are there billions of stars in the universe?*
   Yes, there are.
7. *Is there a cure for the common cold?*
   No, there isn't.
8. *Is there any life on other planets?*
   Maybe. I don't know!

EXERCISE 9

1. There's a picture on the wall.
2. There's a bathroom, a kitchen, and a living room in my house.   (THE RULE GOVERNING ITEM 2 STATES THAT THE VERB BE GENERALLY AGREES WITH THE FIRST NOUN PHRASE THAT FOLLOWS IT.)
3. There are three bedrooms and two bathrooms in the apartment.
4. There is a good restaurant in my neighborhood.
5. There isn't any milk in the refrigerator./There's no milk in the refrigerator.
6. In my picture, there's one woman and two men.
7. There are no women in the restaurant/There aren't any women in the restaurant.
8. Are there any homeless people in your city?

ACTIVITY 1

The picture differences activity can be done in different ways. The suggestion is for students to work with partners describing two variations of the same picture without looking at each other's pictures. Another possibility is to have several sets of five pictures. Students go around the room describing their pictures, trying to find the student who has exactly the same picture.

ACTIVITY 2

You may want to make this into a contest about the most pleasant city to live in. Have students generate additional noun phrases that reflect what they would or would not like to see in a city. Using the information they provide, they choose the most pleasant city. They could also make up a travel brochure specifying the characteristics of the various places represented by the class.

ACTIVITY 3

You may want to include other categories you think are appropriate for your class, such as religion, political affiliation, etc.

ACTIVITY 4

Perhaps students could bring in pictures of the places they are describing. Put the pictures on the board so that the students who have drawn the places can try to find them at the end.

ACTIVITY 5

This could also be done in the context of a letter home to family or friends, or a more formal letter to the Mayor of the city in question.

UNIT 1

The Verb *Be*
Affirmative Statements; Subject Pronouns

The verb BE is dealt with in the first three units of this book since there is a lot of information to be presented. This first unit deals with the context of nationalities, countries, and ethnicity. Putting a large world map in the front of the room so students could locate the countries mentioned in the task as well as their own would enhance the lesson. You might want students to fill out their personal information on real index cards in preparation for Activity 4.

The photographs in the task show people in the context of their respective countries in order to help students match the photo to the text. You might put the information about the people in the photographs on separate index cards and then place the cards on the world map so students could do the same later on when asked for personal information.

Task

1. C
2. D
3. A
4. B

Focus 1

To further clarify the notions of Asian, Hispanic, Latino, or Middle Eastern, ask students to identify their ethnicity.

Exercise 1

1. Natalia
2. is
3. Fernando
4. is
5. Fernando and Young Soon
6. Korea
7. is
8. Colombia
9. Russia
10. are
11. Fernando
12. Natalia

Focus 2

Make sure students understand anaphoric reference: that is, how the subject pronoun is used to refer to the noun phrase in the previous sentence. This will help when students deal with object pronouns used for reference in later units.

Exercise 2

1. <u>They</u> are Asian.
2. <u>It</u> is in the Pacific Ocean.
3. <u>He</u> is from Cyprus.
4. <u>You</u> are Turkish.
5. <u>She</u> is Korean.
6. <u>It</u> is in the Caribbean.
7. <u>We</u> are French.
8. <u>You</u> are Brazilian.
9. <u>I</u> am American.

Exercise 3

This is the first *Information Gap Exercise* in the book. In this particular **information gap,** students have different information and have to transmit the information orally to their partners so their partners can complete the chart. Make sure students know how to execute this exercise.

Have two students demonstrate how to do the exercise in front of the class to show the others how to work. Students can work in pairs and then check their answers by looking at their partner's chart. Note that the names in List B are divided into male and female so that Student B needs to listen to the statement with the name, scan the list to find the name on his or her chart, and then make a statement with the appropriate subject pronoun.

LIST A:

Name	Country	Nationality
Rodrigo	Argentina	*Argentinean*
Carla	*Italy*	Italian
Miguel	*Brazil*	Brazilian
Hiromi	Japan	*Japanese*
Mohammed	*Morocco*	Moroccan
Ivonne	Venezuela	*Venezuelan*
Chin Hui	*Taiwan*	Taiwanese
Kyong Ho	*Korea*	Korean
Michele	France	*French*
Amir	Israel	*Israeli*
Pany	*Greece*	Greek
Muhsin	*Turkey*	Turkish
Bernice	The Dominican Republic	*Dominican*
Stefanie	Germany	*German*
Ashi	*Iran*	Iranian

LIST B:

Name	Country	Nationality
Males:		
Muhsin	Turkey	*Turkish*
Miguel	Brazil	*Brazilian*
Amir	*Israel*	Israeli
Pany	Greece	*Greek*
Rodrigo	*Argentina*	Argentinean
Mohammed	Morocco	*Moroccan*
Females:		
Ashi	Iran	*Iranian*
Chin Hui	Taiwan	*Taiwanese*
Michele	*France*	French
Hiromi	*Japan*	Japanese
Ivonne	*Venezuela*	Venezuelan
Bernice	*The Dominican Republic*	Dominican
Stefanie	*Germany*	German
Carla	Italy	*Italian*
Kyong Ho	Korea	*Korean*

Exercise 4

As the class is completing this exercise and making summary statements, have a pair of students put the summary statements on the blackboard or on butcher block paper in the front of the room. In this way, the other students can check their answers and use these when making their own summary statements about the class.

1. One student is from Iran.
2. Three students are Asian. (Taiwan, Japan, Korea)
3. Four students are from Europe. (Italy, Germany, France, Greece)
4. Three students are from South America. (Brazil, Argentina, Venezuela)
5. One student is Central American. (The Dominican Republic)
6. Three students are from the Middle East. (Iran, Turkey, Israel)
7. One student is French.
8. *The answer to this question can be either three or four students are Hispanic. Though Brazilians are speakers of Portuguese, they would most likely be classified as members of the ethnic group "Hispanic" or "Latino; coming from South America."*

Exercise 5

Students may not be familiar with these famous personalities, so use pictures from popular magazines whenever possible. Students might also be asked to make statements or bring in pictures of famous personalities that they know. Encourage them to make any statements they can.

1. Madonna is from the United States.   She's American.
2. Yoko Ono is from Japan.   She's Japanese.
3. Sophia Loren is from Italy.   She's Italian.
4. Arnold Schwarzenegger is from Austria.   He's Austrian.
5. Margaret Thatcher is from Great Britain.   She's British.
6. The Rolling Stones are from Great Britain.   They're British.
7. Luciano Pavarotti is from Italy.   He's Italian.
8. Nelson Mandela is from South Africa.   He's South African.
9. Catherine Deneuve is from France.   She's French.
10. Robert Redford is from the United States.   He's American.

Exercise 6

Students ask five different classmates the questions in Focus 4.

Exercise 7

1. **Frank:** Hello. I'm Frank.
   Philippe: Hello, Frank [or "Nice to meet you, Frank," or "I'm Frank"]. My name is Philippe.
2. **Lilik:** Hi! I'm Lilik. What's your name?
   Alvaro: My name's Alvaro.
   Lilik: Where are you from, Alvaro?
   Alvaro: Venezuela. Where are you from?
   Lilik: I'm from Indonesia.
3. **Michael:** Hi, Gregg. This is Jane.
   Gregg: Hi, Jane! How are you?
   Jane: Fine, thanks. And you?
   Gregg: Great!

Activities

Activities 1 and 2

Put the list of the students in your class on butcher block paper or on the blackboard so that students can write the summary statements requested in Activity 2. Ask students to make statements using percentages (e.g., 75% of the students are Asian.)

Activity 3

This is a fun activity in which students can be very active. Collect all the papers the students write and put them up around the room. Students then walk around and write the name of the student they think wrote the sentences.

UNIT 2

The Verb *Be*
Yes/No Questions;
Be + Adjective;
Negative Statements

Bring in the Classified section of several newspapers to familiarize students with classified ads. Make sure students understand the vocabulary before they try to do the task. Have them work in groups and encourage them to try to do the task without looking in the dictionary. They might know one word that will allow them do the matching. By working in groups, they can pool their knowledge to complete the task.

Task

1. **C**
2. **D**
3. **A**
4. **B**

Focus 1

Both forms of the contraction are presented here. Have students use negative contractions ("No, he isn't.") until Focus 4, where negative statements and contractions with *not* are introduced as being more emphatic.

Exercise 1

Answers may be "Yes, I am/No, I'm not."

Exercise 2

1. **B:** <u>Are</u> you open today?
   A: Yes, <u>we</u> <u>are</u>.
2. **Mitch:** <u>Are</u> you Karen Smith?
   Karen: Yes, <u>I</u> <u>am</u>.
   Mitch: <u>Are</u> <u>you</u> free tonight?
   Karen: No, <u>I'm</u> <u>not</u>.
3. **B:** Yes, <u>it</u> <u>is</u>.
   A: <u>Is</u> Dr. Frend busy?

4. **Hui Chen:** Hello, _is_ this the "Cool School of English"?
   Secretary: Yes, _it_ _is_.
   Hui Chen: _Are_ the classes big?
   Secretary: No, _they_ _aren't_ / _they're_ _not_.
   Hui Chen: _Are_ the teachers experienced?
   Secretary: Yes, _they_ _are_.
   Hui Chen: _Is_ the tuition expensive?
   Secretary: No, _it_ _isn't_ / _it's_ _not_.

Exercise 3

(1) *am*
(2) *am*
(3) *am not/'m not*
(4) *Are*
(5) *Are*   (6) *you*
(7) *Are*   (8) *you*

Exercise 4

Have students start creating their own adjective/opposites list in their notebook. You can also write the adjective on one side of an index card and its opposite on the other side, creating a file with which you could do quick warm-ups at the beginning of the lesson.

1. (a) old
   young

2. (a) strong
   weak

3. (a) happy
   sad

4. (a) overweight
   thin

5. (a) poor
   rich

6. (a) tall
   short

7. (a) beautiful
   ugly

8. (a) angry
   calm

9. (a) lazy
   energetic

10. (a) messy
    neat

11. (a) funny
    serious

12. (a) sick
    healthy

Exercise 5

This is another *Information Gap Exercise* in which one student has all the information and the other student needs to ask yes/no questions in order to complete his or her chart. You might want to have students change roles in the middle (after "**B. Weight**") so that Student B could then be looking at Part C in Chart A and Student A could be filling in answers on Chart B.

Exercise 6

Students ask yes/no questions with the adjectives in Exercise 5.
 Possible questions may include: "Are you tall?" "Are you medium height?" "Are you short?" "Are you thin?" "Are you average weight?"
 Answers will be "Yes, I am," "No, I'm not."

Exercise 7

Students generate statements from the information they collected in Exercise 6.

Focus 3

This focus presents negative statements with *be* using both the *be* contraction and the negative contraction. There is a slight difference between the two in that when the verb *be* is contracted and followed by *not* as a full word, it makes a stronger negative which is used to contradict or correct someone. Although this is not a crucial nuance for beginning level students, it is important to make them aware of this difference and to have them practice it.

Exercise 8

This exercise sets up an authentic context for using the negative contraction of *be*. As it is sometimes difficult to differentiate between a last name (family name) and a first name (given name), students can use the negative contraction here to correct each other.

1. The last name's not Yu-ho. It's Oh./
   The first name's Yu-ho.
2. He's not Korean. He's Taiwanese.
3. He's not 25. He's 23.
4. Yes, he is./That's right.

5. The first name's not Alice. It's Aline.
6. Yes, she is./That's right.
7. She's not from Germany. She's from Holland.
8. She's not 52. She's 32.

9. The first name's not Mafegna. It's Abiy./
   The last name's Mafegna.
10. He's not Italian. He's Ethiopian.
11. Yes, he is./That's right.
12. He's not married. He's single.

13. Jehad's not Jordanian. He's Lebanese.
14. He's not 29. He's 27.
15. Yes, he is./That's right.

Activities

Activity 1

You might want to introduce additional adjectives from picture charts in order to help students with this activity. As students are working in groups, walk around giving them the adjectives they need. Have pairs present their similarities and differences to the class. This activity could be used as a warm-up in the next class, with students working with a different partner. Or you might want to have students change partners several times during the same lesson.

Activity 2

Have students work in small groups of three or four with the goal of trying to find the best woman for Mark. At the end of the allotted time, have a spokesperson in each group tell the class the group's decision and explain it. If other groups disagree, have them express their disagreement using negative contractions.

Activity 3

Compile the personal ads that your students have written and create a newspaper column that you could exchange with another class. Match up students from your class with students from another class. Have the pairs talk about how they are similar and different.

UNIT 3

The Verb *Be*
Wh-Questions

Since the task is testing students' knowledge about places in the world, it would be helpful to have a world map available for students to refer to. The task should open a lot of free discussion and would work best if students worked in groups so they could rely on each other's background knowledge and not feel pressured into answering on their own.

Task

1. Mexico City.
2. In Nepal
3. The Pope.
4. It's cold.
5. In Tibet.
6. The last Thursday in November.
7. 12:00 P.M.
8. North America, South America, Europe, Asia, Africa, Antarctica, Australia
9. Almost 4,700 years old.
10. It's cold because of the angle of the sun's rays.

Exercise 1

Be sure students read the answers before doing the questions.

1. How old
2. Who
3. Where
4. How
5. What
6. When/What
7. What time
8. When
9. Why
10. What

Exercise 2

This is a variation of a Jeopardy™ game. You can have students work in pairs or do this as a team activity in which students are working in groups of three or four so they can pool their ideas and answer the questions. The answers for the last column, "Rivers, Mountains, and Deserts," may vary, since some of these places might not be in one particular country. For example, the Rocky Mountains are found in the United States and in Canada. Students could also answer "in North America." Have a map available for students to refer to. Students could also recycle yes/no questions with *be* here ("Is the Nile River in Egypt?").

Amount $$$	Categories				
	Monuments	Capitals	Countries	Continents	Rivers. Mountains, Deserts
Questions	Where {is... are...	What's the capital of...	Where's...	Where's...	Where {is... are...
$10	It's in Paris. (In Paris.) (Paris.)	Kabul.	In Nicaragua.	In North America.	In Africa.
$20	It's in the People's Republic of China.	Athens.	In Japan.	In South America.	In North America.
$30	It's in Rome.	Jerusalem.	In Hungary.	In Asia.	In South America.
$40	They're in Egypt.	Lima.	In South Africa.	In Africa.	In Nepal.
$50	It's in India.	Ankara.	In Switzerland.	In Europe.	In Africa.

Exercise 3

1. d
2. h
3. e
4. b
5. f
6. a
7. c
8. g

Exercise 4

Answers may vary. Students ask questions using *who* about their classmates. You can make this exercise into a class activity by having students work in teams and write questions with *who* about the class. The team then asks another team a *who* question. If the group answers, they get five points. The object is for the teams to ask difficult questions that the others can't answer.

Focus 2

This is the first Use Box on Communication Strategies in the book. We have introduced it here to teach students how to get information about English. Although these may not be the most idiomatic expressions for asking about English (see Unit 12), it is important that students begin to learn about strategies as early as possible. Try to encourage students to use these strategies in other activities as well. Put these questions up at the front of the room so you can point to them when students need to use them.

Exercise 5

Answers may vary. Have students ask questions about meaning and pronunciation. Encourage students to use these strategies regularly in class.

Exercise 6

This is an *Information Gap Exercise*. It may be fun to have students do this back to back, with each student looking at either Map A or Map B. Give students a map of the United States and have them create their own weather map so they can get further practice using these questions.

Exercise 7

1. It's 10:00 A.M.
2. It's 8:00 P.M.
3. It's 6:00 P.M.
4. It's 11:30 P.M.
5. It's 5:15 A.M.

Activities

Activity 1

Students should have access to a world map or atlas in order to do this activity successfully.

Activity 2

Students may need to have a more detailed map of the United States in order to locate other cities and ask questions.

Activity 3

As a follow-up to this activity, students could orally present what they learned from the classmate they interviewed. Students could also put together a small class newspaper about these cities. As an alternative, they could create posters that would have some realia from their countries along with the texts. Encourage students to bring in maps, photographs, or drawings from their countries. Post them around the room and have an "international day" event.

Noun Phrases
Count and Non-Count Nouns

Task

Both count and non-count nouns have intentionally been included as categories in the task so as not to convey to students that all categories are non-count nouns. It might be useful to make the vocabulary in the task clear to students by bringing in pictures or having students draw on the board.

1. Food
   - **f.** meat
   - **g.** vegetables

2. Clothing (things to wear)
   - **c.** sportswear
   - **g.** shoes

3. Electronic Equipment
   - **b.** TV sets
   - **h.** cameras

4. Transportation
   - **e.** trains
   - **i.** buses

5. Entertainment (things to do)
   - **a.** concerts
   - **d.** movies

Focus 1

Presentations of count/non-count nouns tend to confuse learners when they imply that nouns are inherently count or non-count. In fact, it is how you view the object that determines how you choose the noun. This explains why some nouns can be both count and non-count. Let's take, for example, the noun *fruit*. If you are viewing fruit as a mass — as one entity — you will use it as a non-count noun: ***The fruit in the bowl looked refreshing***. If, on the other hand, you are viewing *fruit* as individual or separate entities, you would use it as a count noun: ***I try to eat at least one fruit a day***. Further discussions of count vs. non-count nouns, and ways of changing non-count into count nouns, can be found in Unit 24 (Quantifiers).

Exercise 1

Count Nouns	Non-Count Nouns
1. vegetables	1. food
2. things to wear	meat
shoes	2. clothing
3. TV sets	sportswear
cameras	3. electronic equipment
4. buses	4. transportation
trains	5. entertainment
5. movies	
concerts	
things to do	

Exercise 2

Fruit	Furniture	Jewelry	Housing
an orange	*an armchair*	*an earring*	*a dormitory*
a banana	*a sofa*	*a watch*	*an apartment*
a pear	*a table*	*an emerald*	*a mobile home*
an apple	*a desk*	*a ring*	*a house*

Exercise 3

1. He's a waiter.
2. He's an actor.
3. She's an athlete.
4. She's a secretary.
5. He's a dentist.
6. He's a flight attendant.
7. She's a nurse.
8. She's an engineer.
9. He's a cashier.
10. She's a doctor.
11. He's a hairdresser.
12. He's a construction worker.

Exercise 4

Students introduce each other using the occupations from Exercise 3.

Exercise 5

For this *"Test your Knowledge"* exercise, it might be useful to have students work in small groups so they can help each other and activate their background knowledge.

1. m. It's a country.
2. g. It's a holiday in the United States.
3. j. It's an ocean.
4. k. It's an island.
5. n. It's a desert.
6. a. It's a continent.
7. f. It's a city.
8. l. It's an airplane.
9. d. It's a clock in London.
10. c. It's a museum.
11. i. It's a university.
12. h. It's an hour.
13. b. It's a car.
14. e. It's a river.

Exercise 6

1. parties
2. shoes
3. boxes
4. bananas
5. chairs
6. glasses
7. wives
8. watches
9. leaves
10. beds
11. months
12. keys

Exercise 7

1. holidays
2. oceans
3. continents
4. universities
5. companies
6. stories
7. mountains
8. countries
9. states
10. cities

Focus 4

Students will have difficulty pronouncing the "iz" plural: *classes, sandwiches,* etc. You may need to devote some extra time to this.

Exercise 8

Use realia such as rulers, one-pound cans of coffee, quart containers, etc., to facilitate this exercise. Students can be asked to make statements comparing the metric system to the English system (e.g., 1 mile = 2.2 kilometers).
(Students can use the verb *equals* or *is*.)

1. One foot equals 12 inches. (One foot is 12 inches.)
2. One pound equals 16 ounces.
3. One minute equals 60 seconds.
4. One hour equals 60 minutes.
5. One day equals 24 hours.
6. One year equals 365 days.
7. One quart equals 2 pints.
8. One gallon equals 4 quarts.
9. One inch equals 2 ½ centimeters.
10. One kilo equals 2.2 pounds.

Exercise 9

Bring in pictures or photographs to show the characters mentioned in this exercise (Big Bird, Mickey and Minnie Mouse, etc.). Students may work in groups to help each other.

1. feet
2. mice
3. women/men
4. deer
5. people
6. teeth
7. children
8. People

Exercise 10

This exercise could provoke a lot of discussion, so after students have worked in pairs or groups, bring the whole class together to share their statements and write them on the blackboard. Students could compare their answers (e.g., *Public transportation is good in Quebec. It's not good in _____.*). You may need to review vocabulary before they begin.

1. Is American music popular in _____?
2. Are bicycles common in _____?
3. Is electricity cheap in _____?
4. Is public transportation good in _____?
5. Are families big in _____?
6. Are taxes high in _____?
7. Is fresh fruit available in _____?
8. Are cars big in _____?
9. Are sandwiches popular in _____?
10. Is housing expensive in _____?
11. Is accurate news about the world available in _____?

Exercise 11

Another variation of this exercise and one in which students could be more active is by having students do an opinion survey. Each student could be given one question (e.g., *Is furniture expensive in _____? How much is a sofa in _____?*). Students would then get up from their seats and walk around the room asking that question to each member of the class. At the end of the exercise, the students could summarize the results and present the statistics to the class (e.g., *Furniture is expensive in Italy, Germany, and Japan. It's not expensive in Colombia and Pakistan.*).

1. a. Is furniture expensive in _____?
   b. How much is a sofa?
2. a. Is public transportation expensive in _____?
   b. How much is a bus ride?
3. a. Is meat expensive in _____?
   b. How much are steaks?
4. a. Is housing expensive in _____?
   b. How much is an apartment?
5. a. Is fruit expensive in _____?
   b. How much is an apple?
6. a. Is entertainment expensive in _____?
   b. How much is a movie?
7. a. Is clothing expensive in _____?
   b. How much are sneakers?
8. a. Is electronic equipment expensive in _____?
   b. How much is a VCR?

Activities

Activity 1

Make sure students understand the categories on the cards before they do the activity. You may want to set a time limit in order to make the game more active and exciting. Another way to do this activity would be to ask students to use other words they can think of besides the words suggested to them. You might also create additional categories that are more appropriate for your students. Additional categories: things that are red, things found in the classroom, things you find in a city, etc. The group with the most items for their categories wins.

Activity 2

Have students work in groups, writing up their lists on large pieces of butcher block paper. Then put the paper up in the front of the room and compare lists. You can have students identify the count and non-count nouns.

Activity 3

Another variation of this activity would be to write the name of a famous person on a card and tape it on a student's back so that the student cannot see what is written. The other students in the class know what is written on the card. The student must ask yes/no questions to find out who he or she is.

UNIT 5

The Verb *Have*
Affirmative/Negative;
Questions and Short Answers;
Some/Any

Task

Although this unit recycles the knowledge of count/non-count nouns gained from Unit 4 on Noun Phrases, there is a good deal of new vocabulary here that you may want to pre-teach in order to enable students to complete the task. Have them work in pairs or groups or as a whole class first to match the names of the items to the corresponding pictures.

The theme of this unit is modern vs. traditional life-styles. Use the pictures to explain the difference between "modern" and "traditional" so that students can make the logical conclusion at the end of the task. Activities 4, 5, and 6 also involve this theme.

For diagnostic purposes, instead of asking students to check *Mary* or *Nilaulaq,* ask students to **produce** the structure — to make statements aloud, or write statements expressing what each woman has. You could also include questions in the diagnostic phase. This will allow you to see if students know the *do* insertion rule for questions and negatives. How much your students already know will dictate how many of the Focus Boxes and Exercises you will decide to work on with them.

1. Mary
2. Nilaulaq
3. Nilaulaq
4. Mary
5. Nilaulaq (or both Nilaulaq and Mary)
6. Nilaulaq
7. Mary
8. Mary
9. Nilaulaq
10. Mary

Exercise 1

1. has
2. has
3. have
4. have
5. have
6. have
7. have
8. has
9. has
10. have

Exercise 2

While practicing the singular and plural forms of *have* in the given context, students draw logical conclusions using the background knowledge they have gained from the text. Even though the structure is built-in (they are using only the affirmative form of *have*), injecting the thought process into the grammar exercise is an attempt to make the repetition of the structure more meaningful and to prepare students for further exercises in which they are called upon to provide their own logical conclusions or thoughts about the information given.

1. (a) has   (b) has   (c) has   (d) has   (e) have   (f) have   (g) have
2. (a) has   (b) has   (c) has
3. (a) has   (b) has   (c) have
4. (a) have   (b) have

Focus 2

This Focus Box shows the difference between *be* and *have*. The structure of *have* is very important, as it will prepare students for the present tense verbs dealt with in Units 11 and 12.

Have can be presented more inductively by asking students to focus first on the chart comparing *be* and *have*. Ask students to state the differences between the two, and try to elicit the rule for negation from them. Then refer them to Focus Box 2.

Exercise 3

Answers, as well as the number of items elicited, may vary. Possible answers include:

1. Nila doesn't have a sewing machine.
2. Nila and Charlie don't have electricity.
3. Nila and Charlie have a canoe.
4. Modern Eskimos don't have igloos.
5. Traditional Eskimo women don't have cameras.
6. Modern Eskimo women have canned food.
7. Tents don't have heat in the winter.
8. A modern town has a school.
9. Mary has a radio.

Focus 3

The important points to emphasize here are:

- that negative contractions are the commonly used form. Full-word negatives are used for emphasis — to contradict or correct; and
- that there is a difference between American and British English: Americans say, "Does he have…?," **not** "Has he…?" (Students tend to produce *has he*… because it follows the pattern they learned in *be* and because it may correspond to what they do in their native languages.)

Exercise 4

In this exercise, the answers cannot be found in the pictures. Students are required to use background knowledge and think about the content before making their statements. It may be necessary to review the new count and non-count noun phrases in this exercise first. Then, have students do the exercise in pairs, in small groups, or as a class, but try to encourage discussion to see how they have arrived at their conclusions. For example: *Nila doesn't have a refrigerator — Nila doesn't have electricity.* This will provide additional opportunities to practice the structure.

1. Q: *Does* Mary *have* a television set?
   A: *Yes, she does. (Maybe.)*
2. Q: *Does* a traditional Eskimo woman *have* a refrigerator?
   A: *No, she doesn't.*
3. Q: *Do* modern Eskimos *have* igloos?
   A: *No, they don't.*
4. Q: *Do* modern Eskimo houses *have* running water?
   A: *Yes, they do.*
5. Q: *Do* modern Eskimos *have* heat in the winter?
   A: *Yes, they do.*

Exercise 5

This exercise provides more open-ended structure practice and gets students up out of their seats, moving around the room, actively seeking information from one another. They get practice in question formation as well as in the use of count/non-count nouns. You may want to add to this list other items of particular relevance to your students.

1. Do you have a cordless telephone?
2. Do you have a pet?
3. Do you have a car?
4. Do you have children?
5. Do you have an English–English dictionary?
6. Do you have jewelry?
7. Do you have a job?
8. Do you have a bicycle?
9. Do you have a library card?
10. Do you have a VCR?

Focus 4

Here we are trying to present not only the difference between *some/any*, but also the nuance in meaning between an affirmative statement with *some* and one without *some*. What we are saying is that an affirmative statement with *some* implies a limited quantity, even though it does not specifically define that quantity. An affirmative statement without *some* does not focus on quantity, but rather on the presence or absence of an item. The same is true for questions with or without *any*.

You may want to try to apply this distinction to Exercise 6. In other words, for number 1, focus on the difference between the following two sentences:

The town theater has American movies.

The town theater has some American movies.

We had intended to include three choices in Exercise 6 — *some* or *any*, or nothing — but felt that this might be confusing to some people. We invite you to try this distinction!

Exercise 6

Students are asked to make value judgments on the statements produced in this exercise. We recommend that you spend time discussing the positive and negative aspects of the "modernization" of traditional cultures. There are no correct answers for this part of the exercise. The goal is to encourage critical thinking and discussion, and perhaps to get students to apply this to the technological, social, culinary, and linguistic changes that may be occurring in their own native countries as a result of foreign influence.

1. some
2. any
3. some
4. any
5. some
6. some
7. any
8. some
9. some
10. any

Exercise 7

This exercise carries through on the theme of traditional cultures by introducing a traditional culture in America — that of the Amish. By forming questions, students are practicing the opposition between singular, plural, and non-count nouns. Although the directions in the students' book say to use *any* with plural count or non-count nouns, it is also acceptable to make these questions without using *any*. Again, as in the case of *some*, there is a nuance in meaning between *"Do Amish people have colorful clothing?"* and *"Do Amish people have any colorful clothing?"* (See Focus 4.)

In addition to the grammar practice, having the students form the questions **before** they read the text will constitute a prereading exercise in which they can form tentative hypotheses on their own or use the pictures to make predictions about the text they are going to read. Then they can read the text and either confirm or disconfirm their hypotheses and predictions. While the text itself is simple and straightforward, it is also the reading process of forming a hypothesis and reading to confirm or refute that hypothesis that is being introduced here. As an activity, you may want to have your students generate other questions and do additional readings about the Amish. See Activity 5.

1. Do Amish people have **(any)** colorful clothing?
2. Do Amish women have **(any)** jewelry?
3. Does an Amish family have a car?
4. Does an Amish home have **(any)** electricity?
5. Does an Amish home have a telephone?
6. Does an Amish family have a television set?
7. Does an Amish child have a computer?
8. Do Amish farmers have **(any)** tractors?
9. Do Amish people have **(any)** horses?
10. Do Amish children have **(any)** special teachers?

Focus 5 and Focus 6

Focus Boxes 5 and 6 deal with two of the communicative uses of *have*. Another communicative use of *have* is talking about sickness or ailments:

I have a headache.

She has a sore throat.

Due to space restrictions, we were unable to include this focus, but we suggest that you do.

Exercise 8

Encourage students to role-play polite requests in complete interactions, as indicated in Focus Box 5.

1. Do you have a match?   *Yes, I do. No, I don't.*
2. Do you have some/any milk?   *Yes, I do. No, I don't.*
3. Do you have a corkscrew?   *Yes, I/we do. No, I/we don't.*
4. Do you have any stamps?   *Yes, I do. No, I don't.*
5. Do you have any change?   *Yes, I do. No, I don't.*
6. Do you have an eraser?   *Yes, I do. No, I don't.*

Exercise 9

You could do this exercise as a dictation instead of simply having students fill in the blanks.

1. John Lapp is Amish.
   He is married./He's married.
   He has long hair.
   He has a long beard.

2. Nilaulaq is an Inuit woman.
   She has long black hair.
   She has a nice smile.

3. Daniel is young.
   He has long blond hair.
   He has bangs.

4. Mary is a modern Eskimo./Mary's a modern Eskimo.
   Mary is happy./Mary's happy.
   She has dark hair.

Exercise 10

This is the first Error Correction exercise in the book. Have students work individually or in pairs to rewrite the sentences. If you have access to an overhead projector, you can have a student or pair of students write their corrected sentences on a transparency, which you can then use to check all answers. You could also have the students write their sentences on butcher block paper or on the blackboard.

1. He *has* a car.
2. She *does not/doesn't have* a house.
3. He *doesn't have* a TV set.
4. He *isn't* married.
5. She doesn't *have* children.
6. Does he *have* a canoe?
7. *Is she* an Eskimo?
8. Excuse me, *do you have (any)* change?

Activities

Activity 4

In this activity, students are asked to tell about people they know who have traditional life-styles; to tell what they have and what they don't have. This can be accomplished in different ways. First, they might simply use background knowledge to discuss a traditional group in their country. Second, you might supply them with pictures of traditional peoples from a source such as *National Geographic* magazine. Third, they might be required to find some material in the library and report to the class.

As alternative to having students report one by one in front of the class, create a "poster session" activity. Have six students at a time post their reports on butcher block paper at different stations around the classroom. They could also display their pictures. The rest of the class would go around from one poster session to another, listening to the various reports, asking questions, etc. Then the roles could be reversed, until each member of the class has had a chance to make a presentation.

Activity 5

Have your students generate other questions they would like to have answered about the Amish. Then bring in excerpts about the Amish that answer these questions. You could organize this as a jigsaw reading activity in which each group has a specific question and the corresponding excerpt. They read the text and try to understand the answer; then, each group shares its information with the rest of the class. This limits the reading they each have to do and increases the interaction between groups working toward completion of the activity. A variation on this would be to send small groups of students to the library with a specific question or questions to research. Then they would each come back and pool their information, thereby achieving a more detailed, coherent view of the Amish by cooperating with each other.

Activity 6

Try to get your students to discuss, in simple terms, the influence of American culture on their own cultures. Discuss, for example, the American things they now find in their countries — jeans, rock music, fast food, etc. Do they think this is a positive or negative influence? Have them express their opinions.

UNIT 6

Possessives

Nouns, Adjectives, and Pronouns; Questions with *Whose*; *A/An* versus *The*

You may want to name the objects before students do the task, although it really is not necessary in this case. Note that item #4 in the task is a toupee, #5 is a clown's nose attached to a string, and #9 is two front teeth.

Task

1. I
2. F
3. E
4. A
5. J
6. H
7. D
8. B
9. C
10. G

Focus 1

We have chosen to present all possessive forms in this unit. There are Focus Boxes and Exercises devoted exclusively to nouns, to adjectives, and to pronouns to provide adequate practice for each form.

Exercise 1

1. It is [It's] Bernie's camera.
2. It's Fred and Monica's baby.
3. They are Jesse, George and Thomas' [*or* Thomas's] kites.
4. It's Stan's toupee.
5. It's Bonzo's nose.
6. They're Simon's glasses.
7. They're Bob, Ted, Carol, and Alice's dogs.
8. It's Leona's necklace.
9. They're Chris' [*or* Chris's] two front teeth.
10. It's Mrs. Wolf's cane.

Exercise 2

1. Bernie's
2. Alice's
3. Simon's
4. people's
5. woman's (*or* lady's)
6. Leona's
7. Stan's
8. clown's
9. Chris' (*or* Chris's)
10. boys'

Exercise 3

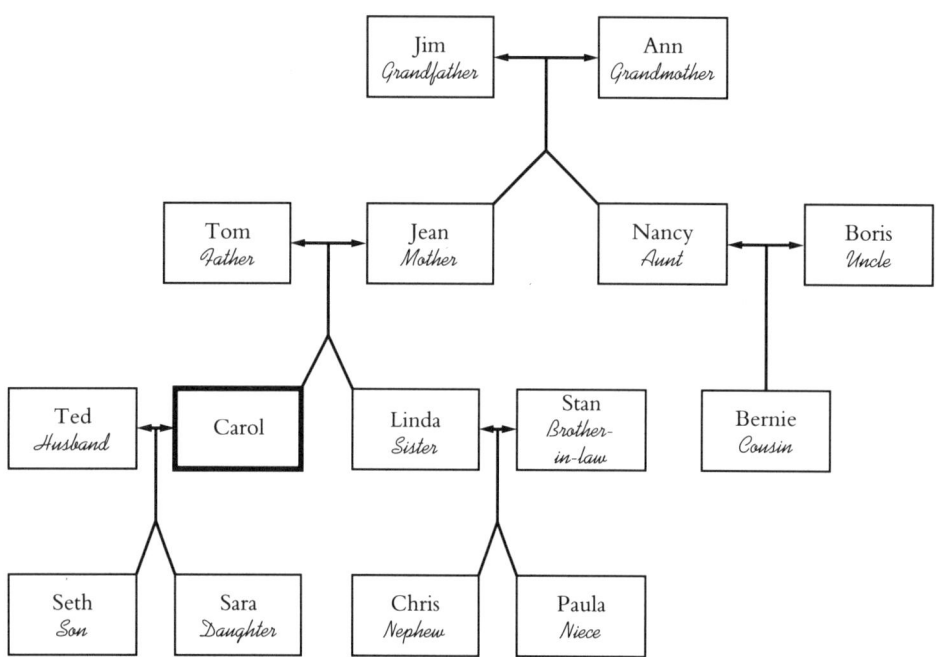

Exercise 4

1. Sara's
2. Bernie's
3. Chris' (*or* Chris's)
4. Linda's
5. Carol and Linda's
6. Bernie's
7. Chris and Paula's
8. Linda and Stan's
9. Ted's
10. Ted and Stan's

Focus 3

FORM

Students often make mistakes with possessive adjectives because they assume that they agree with the noun phrase that follows, not realizing that possessive adjectives are determined by the person who has the thing or relationship. In other words, students will say, "My sister and his husband…" because *husband* is masculine. Make sure too that students understand that possessive adjectives do not function as other adjectives do. In particular, a possessive adjective cannot be preceded by an article.

Exercise 5

1. your
2. I
3. She
4. Her
5. It's
6. your
7. Our
8. It's
9. your
10. My
11. He's
12. His
13. He's
14. My
15. They're
16. We
17. They're
18. We

Exercise 6

This exercise puts students in a situation where they are making inferences using the target structure and the context given.

1. **(g)** His head is bald.
2. **(f)** Her family is rich.
3. **(h)** The missing teeth are her baby teeth.
4. **(i)** Their dogs are lost.
5. **(a)** Their neighborhood isn't very safe.
6. **(d)** His vision is poor.
7. **(b)** His camera is probably made in Japan.
8. **(c)** Their children have children.
9. **(e)** Our [*or* Your] time is up!

Exercise 7

(1) His   (2) His   (3) his   (4) their   (5) her/their   (6) her   (7) my   (8) your   (9) my   (10) his   (11) your

Focus 4

Use pictures from magazines to generate additional vocabulary that might be useful to students (e.g., *Her hair is red, curly, short,* etc.).

Exercise 8

As an entire class activity, students write their names on slips of paper, which are placed in a hat, box, or the like. Each student takes a slip of paper and writes out a description of the person whose name is on the paper. That student then reads the description aloud and the class guesses the person's identity.

Exercise 9

Although we purposely chose these objects for their cultural diversity and interest, some of them may be unfamiliar to the students, especially words such as *saris* and *bowler hats*. Make sure students match the vocabulary to the pictures before doing the exercise. To vary this exercise, students could work in pairs, with one student reading the statement while the second student gives a response using the correct possessive adjective.

1. The chopsticks are hers.
2. The wine and cheese are theirs.
3. The salsa record is his.
4. The McDonald's hamburgers are ours.
5. The hats and umbrellas are theirs.
6. The watches are his.
7. The saris are theirs.
8. The coffee is hers.
9. The tulips are theirs.
10. The trophies are yours.

Exercise 10

1. Whose baby is it? — *It's Fred and Monica's baby.*
   It's theirs.
2. Whose cane is it? — *It's Mrs. Wolf's cane.*
   It's hers.
3. Whose nose is it? — *It's Bonzo's nose.*
   It's his.
4. Whose necklace is it? — *It's Leona's necklace.*
   It's hers.
5. Whose toupee is it? — *It's Stan's toupee.*
   It's his.

6. Whose camera is it?	*It's Bernie's camera.*	
	It's his.	
7. Whose teeth are they?	*They're Chris' [or Chris's] teeth.*	
	They're hers.	
8. Whose kites are they?	*They're the children's [or boy's] kites.*	
	They're theirs.	

Exercise 11

1.	Whose corkscrew is it?	*It's Pierre and Daniel's corkscrew.*	*It's theirs.*
2.	Whose pencil sharpener is it?	*It's Jim's pencil sharpener.*	*It's his.*
3.	Whose lawn mower is it?	*It's John's lawn mower.*	*It's his.*
4.	Whose screwdriver is it?	*It's Jackie's screwdriver.*	*It's hers.*
5.	Whose typewriter is it?	*It's Jim's typewriter.*	*It's his.*
6.	Whose flowerpot is it?	*It's John's flowerpot.*	*It's his.*
7.	Whose hammer is it?	*It's Jackie's hammer.*	*It's hers.*
8.	Whose shovel is it?	*It's John's shovel.*	*It's his.*
9.	Whose saucepan is it?	*It's Pierre and Daniel's saucepan.*	*It's theirs.*
10.	Whose watering can is it?	*It's John's watering can.*	*It's his.*
11.	Whose envelope is it?	*It's Jim's envelope.*	*It's his.*
12.	Whose can opener is it?	*It's Pierre and Daniel's can opener.*	*It's theirs.*
13.	Whose wrench is it?	*It's Jackie's wrench.*	*It's hers.*
14.	Whose paintbrush is it?	*It's Jackie's paintbrush.*	*It's hers.*
15.	Whose spatula is it?	*It's Pierre and Daniel's spatula.*	*It's theirs.*
16.	Whose paper clip is it?	*It's Jim's paper clip.*	*It's his.*

Focus 7

The article system is not always introduced in beginning level ESL texts. However, as stated in our introduction, we believe students will be able to handle this distinction if it is clearly presented as a **discourse choice.** The rules are limited. We use *the* when:

- the Noun Phrase constitutes knowledge shared by the listener or reader (the speaker or writer presupposes this knowledge); or
- the Noun Phrase has already been mentioned (the "given–new contract").

Exercises 12 and 13 demonstrate the use of *a/an* and *the* in discourse. When doing Exercises 12 and 13, have students explain why they chose *a/an* rather than *the,* or vice versa. For instance, in Exercise 13, Example 2, the friend says "**an** air conditioner" because this is the first time the air conditioner has been introduced. The driver, however, says "**the** air conditioner" because the driver is referring to the air conditioner which has already been mentioned.

Exercise 12

(1) a (2) The (3) a (4) a (5) a (6) a (7) the (8) an (9) the (10) a (11) The (12) the (13) the

Exercise 13

1. **(a)** a
2. **(a)** an   **(b)** the
3. **(a)** the **(b)** a   **(c)** the
4. **(a)** a   **(b)** the
5. **(a)** a   **(b)** the
6. **(a)** the **(b)** the
7. **(a)** the
8. **(a)** the

Exercise 14

Error Correction.

1. This magazine is mine.
2. This is Paula's bicycle.
3. Ted is married. Carol is his wife.
4. My eyes are brown.
5. Here is a picture of my family. This is my sister and this is her husband.
6. Is Harry Joan's boyfriend?
7. Whose class are you in?
8. Their children are Bolivian.
9. Michael's car is expensive.
10. The necklace is hers.

Activities

Activity 1

When students have written information about a classmate, they can then compile the stories in a booklet with pictures of the students.

Activity 4

Have students post their family trees around the room. Create a "poster session" in which a few students stand next to their family tree while the rest of the students walk around the room and ask questions about their classmates' family trees.

Activity 6

This activity should promote a lot of discussion about different cultures. Even if you have a culturally homogeneous class, it also provides practice in simply using possessives. If students do not have the actual objects, they can draw them or bring in pictures.

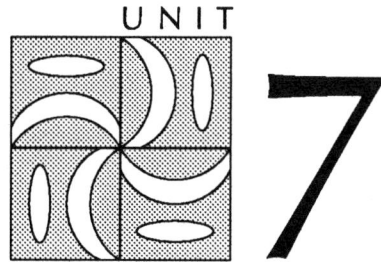

UNIT 7

Demonstratives
Pronouns and Adjectives

Task

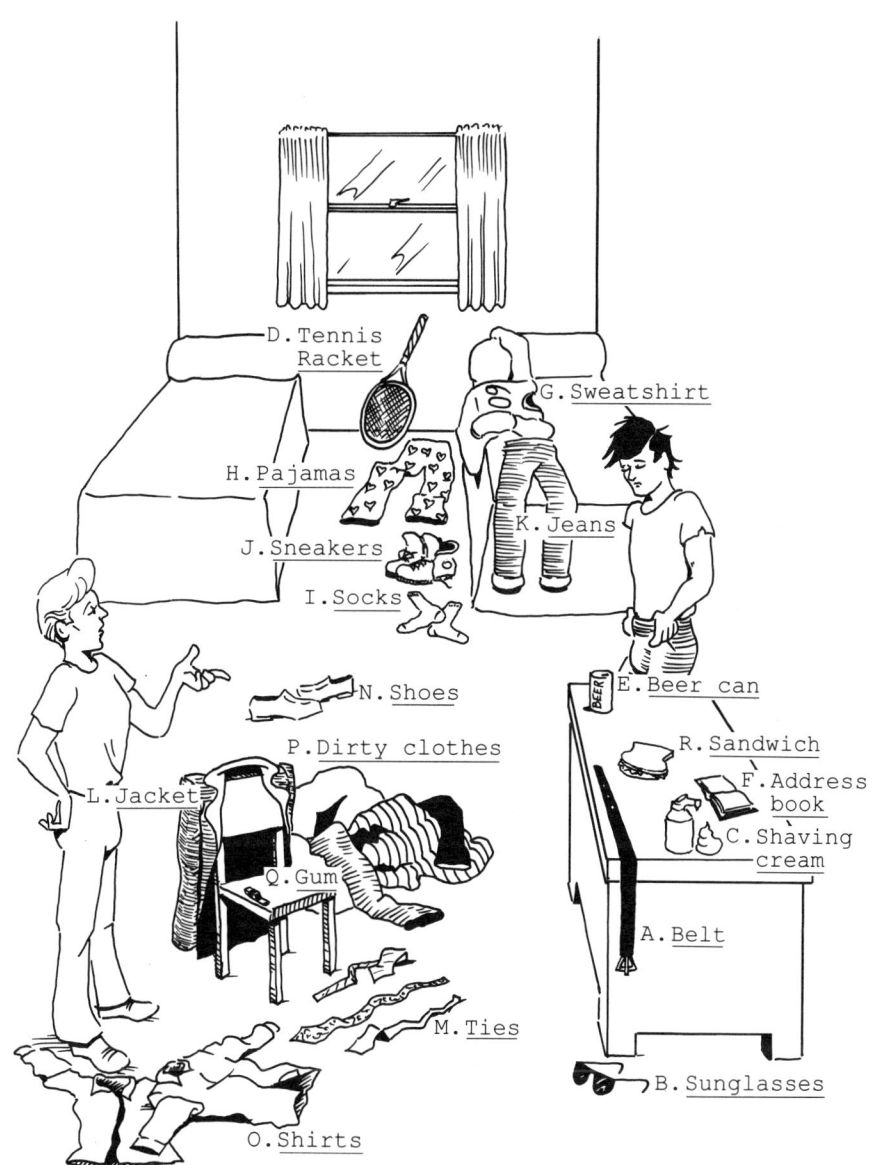

Focus 1

The chart presented in this Focus Box is set up in order to show proximity and distance. It is important to use visuals in this unit to show proximity or distance from the speaker. Start collecting pictures such as flyers from supermarkets and magazine ads. Have students go through magazines and cut out pictures of food, furniture, or clothing items. Place pictures in the room to simulate proximity and distance to help students practice using demonstratives.

Exercise 1

DEMONSTRATIVE PRONOUNS

1. This is my jacket.
2. These are my shirts and ties.
3. These are my sneakers and socks.
4. No, those are yours, Mike.
5. Whose tennis racquet is that?
6. That's your address book.
7. Are those your sunglasses?
8. Whose dirty clothes are these?
9. And is this your gum?

Exercise 3

SINGULAR DEMONSTRATIVE PRONOUNS

<u>This</u> is my jacket.

<u>That</u>'s your address book.

Whose tennis racquet is <u>that</u>?

PLURAL DEMONSTRATIVE PRONOUNS

(These) are my shirts and ties.

(These) are my sneakers and socks.

(Those) are yours.

Are (those) your sunglasses?

Whose dirty clothes are (these)?

DEMONSTRATIVE PRONOUN WITH A NON-COUNT OBJECT

And is **this** your gum?

Exercise 4

1. _That_ _is_ a sweater.
2. _These_ _are_ high-heeled shoes.
3. _This_ _is_ a belt.
4. _Those_ _are_ shorts.
5. _This_ _is_ a dress.
6. _These_ _are_ sunglasses.
7. _That_ _is_ jewelry.
8. _This_ _is_ a skirt.
9. _Those_ _are_ blouses.
10. _This_ _is_ women's clothing.

Exercise 5

1. Just look at this place, Mike.
2. These shoes are mine.
3. That sweatshirt is mine.
4. Are these jeans yours, Ned?
5. What about those pajamas?
6. That belt is yours too.
7. And that shaving cream is yours too.
8. This place is a wreck!

Exercise 6

The vocabulary presented in this exercise might seem too sophisticated for a beginning level class; however, these are items that students see every day when they go shopping for food. The focus on a healthy diet might lead to some interesting discussion as well. If possible, bring in or have students bring in items from the supermarket or cut out ads from supermarket flyers for additional vocabulary. Note that proximity and distance are indicated by arrow length.

1. No, they aren't. _Those cupcakes are fat-free._
2. No, it isn't. _This coffee is decaffeinated._
3. Yes, they are.
4. No, they aren't. _Those popsicles are sugar-free._
5. Yes, it is.
6. Yes, they are.
7. No, it isn't. _This is skim milk._
8. No, it isn't. _That soda is caffeine-free._

Exercise 7

In this exercise, students are also practicing the use of articles with count and non-count nouns introduced in Unit 4.

Letter of the Picture

1. It's a hamburger. (D)
2. It's a hot-dog (frankfurter). (I)
3. They're French fries. (J)
4. It's ketchup. (C)
5. It's pizza (*or* It's a pizza). (F)
6. It's a sandwich. (E)
7. They're doughnuts. (A)
8. They're cookies. (G)
9. It's a muffin. (B)
10. It's ice cream (*or* It's an ice cream cone). (H)

Exercise 8

1. What are those?
2. What is this? (What's this?)
3. What is that? (What's that?)
4. What is this? (What's this?)
5. What are those?
6. What is this? (What's this?)
7. What is this? (What's this?)
8. What is that? (What's that?)

Activities

Activity 2

The activities in this unit are rich in cross-cultural significance. Students can use pictures from magazines or draw the different foods from their countries, and a discussion of different diets and eating habits could ensue.

Activity 3

Bring in a variety of menus — from fast-food restaurants, diners, fine restaurants, etc. Have students work in groups to generate questions. You also could encourage students to find native speakers to talk about the items from a certain menu. The students can come back to class and report on what they learned.

Activity 4

Having students bring in objects from their countries can also stimulate discussions about culture and cultural values. Students are bound to be interested in explaining and sharing important personal or cultural items with their classmates. You might want to have a cultural "fair," with students displaying their items and talking about them.

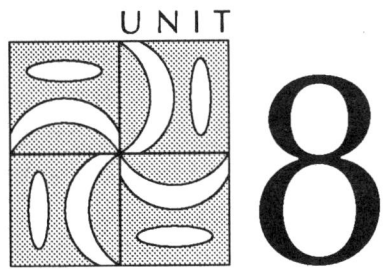

UNIT 8

Be + Prepositional Phrase; *Where* Questions

Task

Have students talk about the picture in the task and identify some of the items they already know before they read the dialogue.

Exercise 1

George: Honey, where's the peanut butter?

Judy: It's **(** (in) the cupboard **)** **(** (above) the stove **)** .

George: Oh, and where are the kids' lunch boxes?

Judy: **(** (In) the cabinet **)** , **(** (under) the sink **)** .

George: Now, where is the plastic wrap?

Judy: **(** (On) the counter **)** , **(** (next to) the toaster **)** .

George: What's next? Oh, the cheese. I know that's **(** (in) the refrigerator **)** . Now what about some fruit?

33

Tommy: No, we want cookies!

George: Judy — where are the cookies?

Judy: They're ((in) the cabinet) ((against) the wall).

George: O.K., kids, we're all ready to go. Where are your jackets?

Tommy: They're ((in) the closet), Dad.

George: Cindy, do you have your books?

Cindy: Yes, Dad. They're ((in) my backpack).

George: What's left? Oh, the keys! Judy, where are the car keys?

Judy: They're ((on) the wall), ((behind) the bird cage).

George: Oh, of course! Now, one more thing. Where are my glasses?

Tommy & Cindy: They're right ((on) your head), Dad!

Exercise 3

Use actual objects in class to introduce the prepositions in this exercise.

  2. A.   5. B.
  1. C.   6. D.
  3. E.   4. F.

Exercise 4

Students generate sentences about objects in the classroom. This exercise can be turned into a game, the goal of which is to write as many sentences as possible for the others to guess.

Exercise 5

1. D
2. E
3. B
4. C
5. A

Exercise 6

This is an *Information Gap Exercise*. It is important that students work in pairs, with one student looking at Picture A and the other looking at Picture B. Have students identify the objects before they ask questions about them. The objects from #1 to #6 are a pair of slippers, a handbag, a pair of gloves, a comb, a hair dryer, and a mug. In Picture B, the objects are a book, a newspaper, an umbrella, a pair of glasses, a pen, and a pair of socks. It might be fun to have students sit back to back while doing this exercise. After they have drawn the objects in their picture, the students could then check their drawings against the original picture.

Exercise 7

Familiarize students with the map and the names of streets and avenues. This could be done as a listening exercise in which you say the sentences and students fill in the places on the map. Alternatively, you could have students work in pairs, with one student reading the sentences aloud to the other.

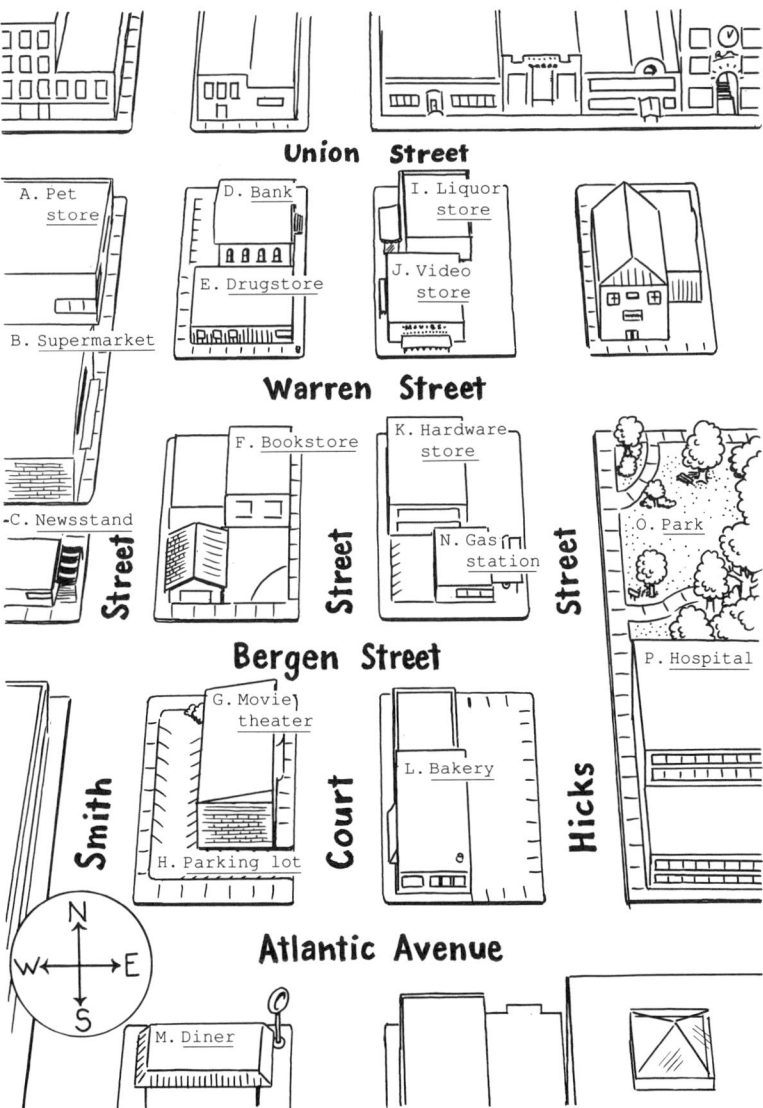

Activities

Activity 2

Give each pair or group of students some felt-tip pens and a large sheet of butcher block paper on which they can draw their (hometown) map. Each student can affix his or her paper to the wall and then present the map to the class, so that students can write down all the prepositional phrases they hear. You can even turn this into a competition in which the student who has the most prepositional phrases wins.

Activity 3

Have six students post their bedroom plans around the room so that the rest of the students can walk around and hear about each bedroom plan. To vary this activity, you can have students draw plans of typical bedrooms in their native countries. This will lead to a discussion of cultural differences.

UNIT 9

Intensifiers
Be + Adjective + Noun

Task

In this task, students are responding subjectively, so there are no definitive answers. Discussion should ensue. To set this task in motion, it's worth spending a couple of minutes with the entire class discussing the usefulness of the different items. Then put students in groups to discuss more specifically how useful and necessary each object is to them.

Exercise 1

Answers will vary. Students generate sentences with intensifiers about the items in the task. One way to do this exercise, varying what was done in the task, would be to write each intensifier on large paper and post each on one of the four walls of the classroom so that the classroom would look like this:

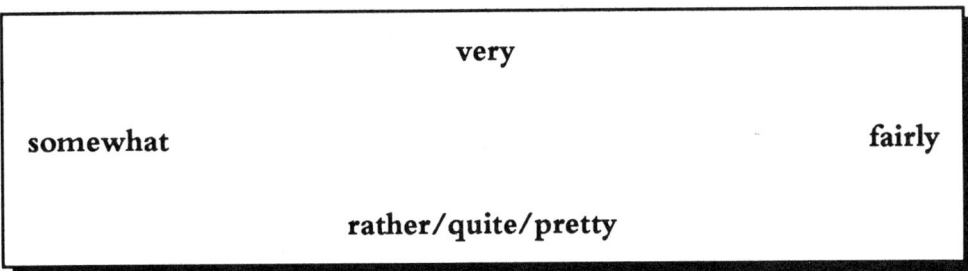

The teacher asks a question such as "How necessary is a computer?" The students then walk to the side of the room that has the intensifier they would use in their answer and make statements using the intensifiers.

Exercise 2

Students would benefit by doing this exercise individually first. They could then be put into pairs or groups to compare their answers. Answers may vary. Possible sentences include:

1. A portable telephone is pretty convenient.
2. Sneakers are very comfortable.
3. French restaurants are rather expensive.
4. A gold necklace isn't very cheap.
5. A vacuum cleaner is very useful.
6. A dishwasher is fairly practical.
7. An encyclopedia is very informative.
8. A word processor is rather efficient.
9. A big car isn't very economical.
10. American movies aren't very popular/are somewhat popular in my country.

Exercise 3

You might want to put different mystery objects in a paper bag (or pictures of different items in case they are too large for the bag) for students to pick out and describe to the class.

1. Spaghetti
2. Beer
3. A toaster
4. A bicycle (*or* A bike)
5. Ice

Exercise 4

Answers to this exercise will vary. For example:

1. My father is very serious. He's somewhat quiet. He's fairly confident.

Encourage students to use additional adjectives if they want to.

Exercise 5

1. c.
2. d.
3. e.
4. a.
5. g.
6. f.
7. b.

Focus 3

This is an important rule for speakers of languages such as Spanish, who will tend to use Noun–Adjective instead of Adjective–Noun. You may want to reinforce the word order by playing games that require unscrambling. For example, write each word of a *Be* + Adjective + Noun sentence on an index card and have students put the cards in the correct order.

Exercise 6

You may need to explain to students that in this conversation, Bernice is Dominican. To check their comprehension, ask students why Carol says, "Of course, they are, if they're like you."

1. It is [It's] a very beautiful country.
2. What is [What's] the capital like?
3. It is [It's] a very big city.
4. It's very crowded, but it is pretty [*or* quite *or* fairly] clean.
5. How high is the inflation?

6. It is [It's] fairly high.
7. What are they like?
8. Dominicans are pretty friendly people.
9. It is [It's] a very interesting place.

Exercise 7

Answers may vary. Possible answers include:

1. The Twin Towers are very tall [or high] buildings in New York.
2. Disney World is a pretty/very exciting/crowded/popular place.
3. Pavarotti is a very talented singer.
4. *Rambo* is a very violent/popular movie.
5. A Mercedes is a very expensive/popular car.
6. A bowl of granola is a fairly nutritious/satisfying meal.
7. Baseball is a very popular/exciting sport in Japan.
8. Tokyo is a very crowded city. Tokyo isn't a very dangerous city.
9. Scuba diving is a rather dangerous/popular sport.
10. Teaching is a fairly satisfying [or exciting] profession.

Activities

Activity 1

Students may need to be introduced to additional adjectives in order to execute this activity successfully. These adjectives might be useful: *heavy, light, wooden* (or *made of wood*), *(made of) metal, (made of) glass,* etc.

Activity 2

You may want to prepare students for the interviews by having them generate and practice all the possible questions for each of the categories. They would then feel more confident in interviewing three different people in class. In a later class, have students bring in pictures of the place they talked about so they can report to the class.

Activity 3

Students should work individually to check the adjectives that describe them and then write the appropriate intensifier.

UNIT 10 — There + Be

Answers to this Unit on *there*, as well as an in-depth explanation on how to use the Unit, can be found at the beginning of the Instructor's Manual on page viii.

UNIT 11

Simple Present Tense
Affirmative and Negative Statements; Time Expressions; In/On/At; Make and Do

You may be surprised to find that the simple present is introduced before the present progressive in this book. The present progressive, being more tangible and easier to demonstrate, tends to be dealt with first in low-level grammars. However, as a result of this sequencing, learners may overgeneralize the present progressive and fail to understand and learn the uses of the simple present. Thus, in this book, the simple present precedes the present progressive.

Task

This is the first piece of extended discourse in the book. As a prereading exercise, ask students to talk about the two pictures and predict the life-styles of each of the two families. Write relevant verbs or lexical items on the board. You might want to discuss the issue of healthy life-styles before they read as well, and have them make predictions that will be confirmed or refuted through reading.

Exercise 1

THE LOWES

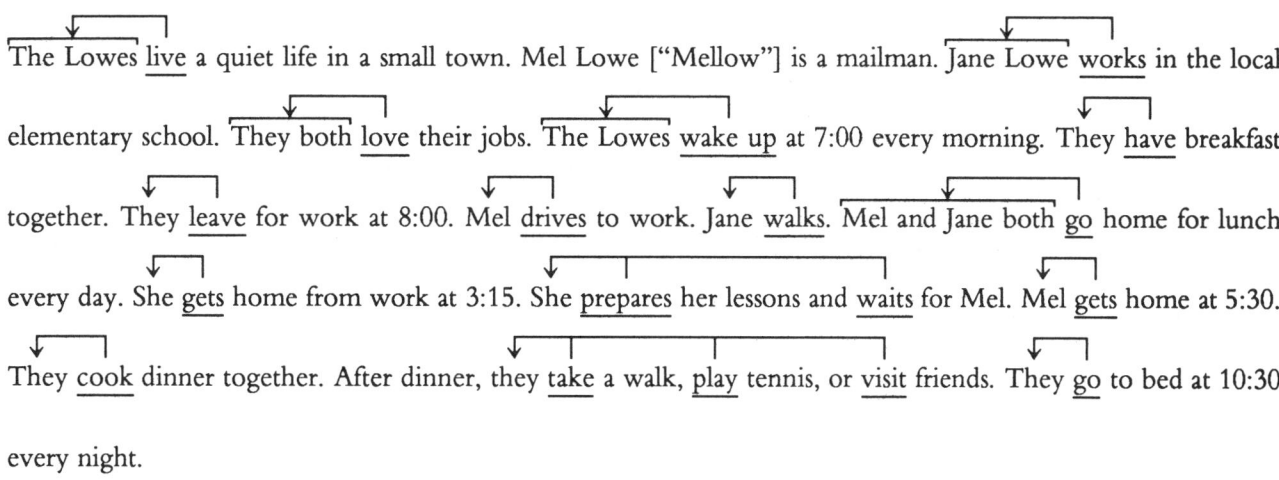

The Lowes live a quiet life in a small town. Mel Lowe ["Mellow"] is a mailman. Jane Lowe works in the local elementary school. They both love their jobs. The Lowes wake up at 7:00 every morning. They have breakfast together. They leave for work at 8:00. Mel drives to work. Jane walks. Mel and Jane both go home for lunch every day. She gets home from work at 3:15. She prepares her lessons and waits for Mel. Mel gets home at 5:30. They cook dinner together. After dinner, they take a walk, play tennis, or visit friends. They go to bed at 10:30 every night.

THE TICKS

The Ticks <u>lead</u> a busy life in the big city. Fran Tick ["Frantic"] is a banker, and her husband Fred is a lawyer. Every day they <u>get up</u> at 6:30. They <u>skip</u> breakfast. They <u>leave</u> home at 7:00. Fred <u>rushes</u> to the subway station. Fran <u>takes</u> a cab to the bank. Fred <u>sees</u> his clients all day. At 12:00, he <u>has</u> a business lunch with a client. They <u>have</u> a cocktail, <u>eat</u> a big lunch, and <u>smoke</u> cigars. He <u>finishes</u> work at 8:00. Fran <u>discusses</u> money problems every day. She <u>leaves</u> work at 8:00 too. She <u>feels</u> hungry and tired. She <u>meets</u> Fred every evening at 8:30. They <u>order</u> in food from the neighborhood restaurant. After dinner, they <u>work</u> in their office at home. They <u>go</u> to sleep at 1:00 A.M. every night.

Exercise 2

1. delivers
2. works
3. love
4. takes
5. walks
6. prepare
7. talks
8. manages
9. stay
10. eat

Focus 2

This Use Box focuses on using the simple present to talk about habits and routines. In order to get the idea of habits and routines across to students, have them generate other examples spontaneously. Write their statements on the board.

Exercise 4

Answers may vary. Students make true statements about themselves using the expressions. Pay attention to word order problems such as "I every year take a vacation."

Focus 4

This Focus Box deals with the spelling and pronunciation of the third person singular form of the simple present tense. Pronunciation is a challenging aspect of this tense, and students should spend time on it. Explain the difference between voiced and voiceless sounds to students by having them put their hands on their throats to feel the vibration that a voiced sound creates.

Exercise 5

You may want to introduce some vocabulary before asking students to do the exercise. Possible vocabulary items include: *to snore, to have trouble sleeping, to go jogging, park bench, to wake someone up, to shake, to scream, to lie down*. Then have students talk either as a class or in groups about what is going on and put the pictures in order. The pictures have been labeled in the correct sequence as follows:

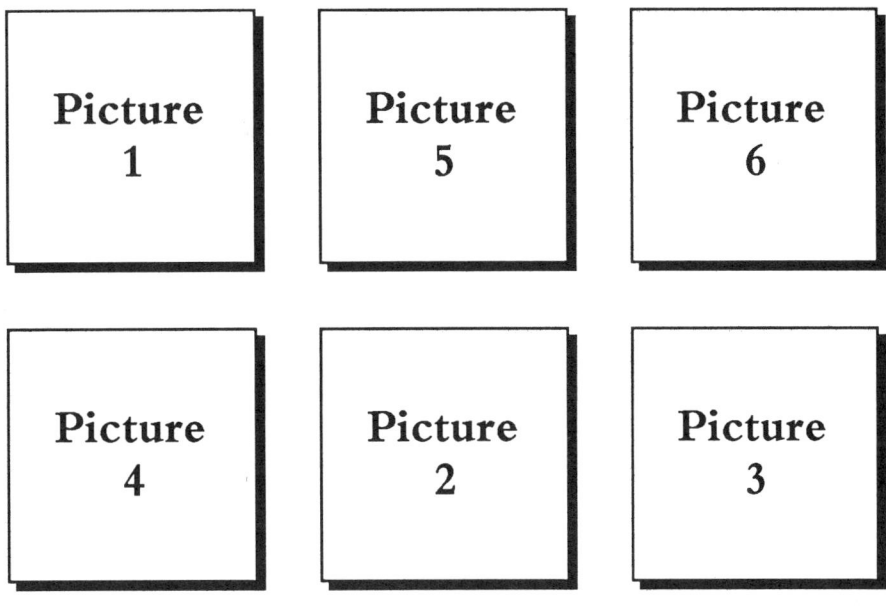

```
  4   A.
  6   B.
  3   C.
  1   D.
  5   E.
  2   F.
```

Another way to do this exercise would be to enlarge the pictures and put each picture on a card. Students can work in groups of six. Each student has one card and describes his or her picture to the group. After hearing all the descriptions, the group tries to put the pictures into the correct order. In a more inductive approach, you could try having your students work in groups to put the pictures in the correct sequence and write a story **before** looking at the text. Have them display their stories on the board or on butcher block paper first, and correct them. Then have students compare their stories to the one given.

Exercise 6

Due to lack of space, we were unable to provide a complete chart for Exercise 6. You may want to reproduce a large chart for the class.

	Verb	/S/	/Z/	/IZ/		Verb	/S/	/Z/	/IZ/
1.	loves		✓		11.	pushes			✓
2.	smiles		✓		12.	leaves		✓	
3.	snores		✓		13.	goes		✓	
4.	wakes	✓			14.	jogs		✓	
5.	shakes	✓			15.	runs		✓	
6.	screams		✓		16.	finds		✓	
7.	hates	✓			17.	lies		✓	
8.	wants	✓			18.	covers		✓	
9.	gets	✓			19.	feels		✓	
10.	puts	✓							

Focus 5

The distinction based on general to specific may help students remember how to use these three prepositions. This also works for prepositions of time (e.g., *in the summer, in 1993, on Tuesday,* and *at 7:00*).

Exercise 7

1. wakes up
2. four days/times a week; on Monday(s), Tuesday(s), Wednesday(s), and Thursday(s); from Monday to Thursday
3. goes out for breakfast/attends meetings/cleans her apartment
4. teaches French
5. at 9:30 (A.M.)
6. two days/times a week; twice a week; (on) Monday and Wednesday; (on) Mondays and Wednesdays
7. (on) Friday; (on) Fridays
8. plays tennis
9. (on) Tuesday; (on) Tuesdays; once a week; at 6:00 on Tuesday
10. on Wednesday; on Wednesdays; on Wednesday nights; once a week
11. goes out with friends

12. four days/times a week; (on) Monday(s), Tuesday(s), Wednesday(s), and Thursday(s); from Monday to Thursday
13. goes to bed
14. (on) Monday; (on) Mondays; once a week; Monday(s) at 8:00 (P.M.)
15. prepares lessons

Exercise 8

Have students also indicate whether the preposition is more general or specific to reinforce the information in Focus 5.

1. at
2. on
3. in
4. on
5. at
6. in
7. on
8. on
9. at
10. on

Exercise 9

Answers will vary. Students generate their own sentences.

Focus 6

The "do" support rule was presented in Unit 5. Elicit the rule from students and have them apply it to present tense before focusing on this Focus Box.

Exercise 10

Answers will vary. Students generate their own sentences about their daily routines.

Focus 7

A different use of the simple present is introduced here: making generalizations. Have students brainstorm other examples, perhaps even about the classroom, teachers, or themselves!

Exercise 11

Answers may vary. Possible answers include:

A healthy person...

2. watches his or her diet.
3. doesn't smoke.
4. eats fruit and vegetables.
5. doesn't worry all the time.
6. finds time to relax.
7. doesn't use drugs.
8. enjoys life.
9. doesn't sleep only five hours a night.
10. doesn't overeat.
11. exercises.

Focus 8

It is very important for students to know these common expressions with *go*. Another way to practice or review this is to write all the main words of the expressions with *go* on index cards (*store, bed, home, supermarket,* etc.) and mix them up. Then ask students to put the cards in one of the following categories:

Go to the	Go to	Go	Go + Verb + ing

Exercise 12

1. the doctor
2. bed
3. the bank
4. work
5. college
6. the supermarket
7. lunch
8. church
9. jail
10. home

Exercise 13

1. goes swimming
2. goes fishing
3. go hiking
4. go biking
5. goes ice skating
6. goes skiing
7. go jogging
8. go dancing

Focus 9

Before students look at this Focus Box, you can check to see just how much they already know about expressions with *make* and *do*. Put the expressions with *make* and *do* on page 127 on index cards without giving the verbs "Make" or "Do." Have students sort the expressions into "Make" or "Do" piles (as in Focus 8 with "Go"). This also gives students a chance to work in groups and exchange their knowledge without relying on the teacher to impart all the information.

Exercise 14

Students generate their own sentences. Subjects of the sentences may vary. Verb form may change depending on the subject (e.g., *My brothers do the dishes* or *My brother does the dishes*).

1. do the dishes
2. make the bed
3. make breakfast
4. make lunch
5. make dinner
6. make the decisions
7. make vacation plans
8. do my homework
9. do the laundry
10. do the shopping

Exercise 15

1. She smiles every day.
2. He takes a walk every day.
3. He finishes his dinner every night.
4. He doesn't cook dinner on Sundays.
5. We study in the library on Saturdays.
6. She doesn't work on Tuesdays.
7. We go shopping every week.
8. She doesn't go to school on Thursdays.
9. She goes jogging on Mondays *or* She doesn't go jogging on Mondays.

Activities

Activity 2

Make this an entire class activity by writing the time expressions on butcher block paper and posting them on different walls around the room. Students could mill around and write a sentence under each time expression. Finally, students could decide which of their habits are unique and which are shared by others.

Activity 3

In order to facilitate this activity, you may want to provide students with some categories for which they can generate statements about habits in their native countries. For example, you might choose: eating, education/schooling, tipping, recreation, work.

Activity 4

You can involve the entire class in this activity by having these categories on large pieces of newsprint around the room. Students could walk around the room and write sentences for each category. You could then either work on errors or point out students' similarities and differences.

Simple Present Tense
Questions; Adverbs of Frequency

The theme of this unit is habits in general, and language learning habits and strategies in particular. Language learning is introduced as a theme here in order to raise the students' awareness of what good language learners do, and to help them analyze their own behavior as language learners.

We have already suggested having students keep a learning journal throughout the semester. After completing this unit, students should have more categories by which to judge themselves and a clearer understanding of themselves as language learners.

Task

You may find it necessary to go over the key vocabulary items in the reading before asking students to complete the task.

1. Yes
2. No
3. No
4. Yes
5. Yes
6. Yes
7. Yes
8. Yes
9. No
10. No

Exercise 1

This exercise points out many of the positive behaviors you want to instill in your students to make them more successful, more autonomous learners, and one negative behavior — avoidance. You will probably want to go through each item to ensure comprehension before beginning the exercise. We recommend open sharing and discussion of the findings. You may want to ask the class to decide who the best language learner is. The learner strategies and styles presented in this unit should be rediscussed periodically throughout the course.

1. Do you speak English outside of class?
2. Do you find different ways to say things when people don't understand you?
3. Do you practice pronunciation?
4. Do you ask people to correct your English?
5. Do you ask questions about English?
6. Do you watch TV in English?
7. Do you guess the meanings of new words?
8. Do you make lists of new words?
9. Do you read something in English every day?
10. Do you write something in English every day?
11. Do you try to understand how English works?
12. Do you avoid English?

Exercise 2

This exercise focuses on the **affective** dimension of learning: attitudes, the role of anxiety and self-esteem, motivation and cooperation (see #1, #2, #3, #4, #8, #9, and #10). It also implicitly introduces three categories of **learning styles:** the *analytic vs. global* and the *sequential vs. intuitive* aspects of style determine whether a learner is detail-oriented or holistic; dependent on a step-by-step presentation of the language or able to think in a more abstract way, figuring out how the language works (see #5). The sensory preference of the learners determines whether they require **visual or auditory** modalities for learning (see #6 and #7).

By working through the *Information Gap,* students are exposed to this information about learning and can relate it to their own learning behavior. You may want to have students ask each other these questions and answer them.

1. Does {Sophia / Mohammed} like English? — Yes, she does. / No, he doesn't.
2. Does {Sophia / Mohammed} need English? — Yes, she does. / Yes, he does.
3. Does {Sophia / Mohammed} think English is difficult? — No, she doesn't. / Yes, he does.
4. Does {Sophia / Mohammed} study with other students? — Yes, she does. / No, he doesn't.
5. Does {Sophia / Mohammed} think grammar is important? — Yes, she does. / Yes, he does.
6. Does {Sophia / Mohammed} learn more by speaking and listening to English? — Yes, she does. / No, he doesn't.
7. Does {Sophia / Mohammed} learn more by reading and writing English? — No, she doesn't. / Yes, he does.
8. Does {Sophia / Mohammed} feel good using English? — Yes, she does. / No, he doesn't.
9. Does {Sophia / Mohammed} have any American friends? — Yes, she does. / No, he doesn't.
10. Does {Sophia / Mohammed} feel bad about making mistakes in English? — No, she doesn't. / Yes, he does.

Exercise 3

This exercise elicits discussion of students' personal habits in preparation for Activity 2, where they will be trying to find a compatible roommate in the class. Encourage students to ask each other additional questions that would be relevant in their decision-making.

1. Do you smoke?
2. Do you drink alcohol?
3. Do you listen to loud music?
4. Do you cook?
5. Do you have parties on weekends?
6. Do you make friends easily?

7. Do you go to bed late?
8. Do you talk on the telephone all the time?
9. Do you study hard?
10. Do you clean your apartment every week?

Exercise 4

This exercise is about school habits in different countries. You may decide to expand this exercise into a discussion. Some topics that may come up are the segregation of boys and girls in school, the teaching of religion, and the cost of education. Ask students to elaborate on these themes, perhaps writing one or two statements about each, and then sharing this information with the class.

1. Does a child start school at age five?
2. Do students wear uniforms to school?
3. Do boys and girls go to separate schools?
4. Do children go to school on Saturdays?
5. Do students study religion in school?
6. Does a student take difficult exams after high school?
7. Does college cost a lot of money?
8. Does the government pay for higher education?
9. Do parents pay for their children's education?
10. Do students work after school?

Focus 2

Since the meanings of adverbs of frequency are very relative, it is difficult to assign percentages to all of them. As you can see, they are presented in order of decreasing frequency.

Exercise 5

This exercise presents a context in which students are required to reflect on their own learning habits and assign an adverb of frequency to each one. Remember that, at this point, they have not yet seen how to position these adverbs. For this reason, the exercise only requires them to understand the meaning of the adverbs and check off the appropriate box. In Exercise 7, they will be asked to produce statements using adverbs of frequency.

Answers for Exercise 5 are personal and will vary.

Exercise 6

This exercise focuses on the meaning of adverbs of frequency in the context of language-learning strategies. The answers are derived from context.

1. always
2. never
3. usually
4. seldom
5. sometimes
6. never
7. usually
8. always

Exercise 7

Students' answers will vary. Check for correct positioning of adverbs of frequency.

Exercise 8

The answers are not complete sentences. For **(e)**, make sure students understand how to use *because* in a short answer and in a complete sentence.

(e) 1.
(g) 2.
(d) 3.
(f) 4.
(b) 5.
(a) 6.
(c) 7.

Exercise 9

This exercise is taken from a non-native TESOL graduate student's journal. It expresses the frustration, anger, and embarrassment so common to students learning English. You could ask your students to write the questions first and then find the answers in the text. Encourage them to verbalize their own frustrations and problems in using English.

1. Where does Carla come from?

   She comes from Haiti.
   She's from Haiti.
   From Haiti.
   Haiti.

2. How does Carla feel when she speaks English?

   She feels embarrassed.
   Embarrassed.

3. Why does Carla feel this way?

   She feels this way because sometimes people don't understand her when she speaks.
   ...because people don't understand her when she speaks.

4. What does Carla want to be?

   She wants to be a bilingual teacher.

5. How often does Carla speak English?

   She seldom speaks English.

6. Why does Carla feel angry?/Why is Carla angry?

   She feels angry because she says Americans only speak English. Americans don't understand the problems people have learning a new language.

Exercise 10

Students will provide their own information to answer these questions.

Focus 6

Although *whom* seems to be disappearing in everyday English, it is still important for learners to know the subject/object distinction.

Exercise 11

This exercise gives students practice in the use of *who* in subject position. As a follow-up to Unit 11, this exercise can stimulate discussion of male and female roles in the family. Encourage students to add items to this list.

1. Who earns money in your family?
2. Who makes important decisions in your family?
3. Who takes out the garbage?
4. Who takes care of the children?
5. Who cleans the house?
6. Who goes shopping?
7. Who is the boss?
8. Who pays the bills?

Exercise 12

1. Who
2. Who
3. Who
4. Whom/Who
5. whom
6. Who
7. whom
8. Who

Focus 8

This Focus Box attempts to further students' knowledge of the communication strategies introduced in Unit 3. These strategies allow them to learn more language while keeping the conversation going. They need to know how to compensate for their lack of linguistic knowledge, either by asking questions about English in appropriate, accurate ways, or by using strategies such as circumlocution to make themselves understood somehow. We have tried to link communication strategies to particular grammar structures throughout the text. These strategies should be reinforced in class whenever possible.

Exercise 13

1. How do you pronounce *language?*
2. What does the word *guess* mean?/What does *guess* mean?
3. How do you say the opposite of *fat?*
4. How do you spell *communicate?*
5. What does the word *strategy* mean?/What does *strategy* mean?

Exercise 14

1. Does he read books?
2. Are they good students?
3. What does *routines* mean?
4. I sometimes watch TV./I watch TV sometimes./Sometimes I watch TV.
5. How often do you listen to native speakers of English?
6. Does he study in the library?
7. What does the class do on Mondays?
8. How do you say "not correct"?
9. I never make mistakes.
10. Why do you feel embarrassed to speak English?

Activities

Activity 1

For this activity, you may want to have students do some reading on the good language learner. Possible sources: *Learner Strategies in Language Learning*, by Anita Wenden and Joan Rubin (Prentice-Hall Language Teaching Methodology Series, 1987); and *How to Be a More Successful Language Learner*, by Joan Rubin and Irene Thompson (Heinle & Heinle, 1982). In addition, any insights gained from the students in the course of this unit could be incorporated in the questionnaire on learning strategies. It would be interesting for students to be able to administer this questionnaire to another class, or interview another group.

Activity 4

This is a good opportunity for students to exchange cultural information. You may want to assist them in this activity by first conducting a brainstorming session in which they come up with categories. They might choose male/female roles, student/teacher classroom behavior, dating habits, etc.

Imperatives

Task

While it may be easy for students to learn to form imperatives, they will often use them inappropriately; and inappropriate use of imperatives can lead to misunderstanding, even hostility. Since the challenge in imperatives lies in Use, the task starts out by presenting some of the Uses of the imperative in various social situations.

Allow students to spend some time discussing what is happening in each cartoon before they match them to the statements.

(a) 6
(b) 4
(c) 2
(d) 5
(e) 3
(f) 1

Exercise 1

(a) Please <u>give</u> me change for a dollar, Sir.

(b) <u>Have</u> a piece of cake with your coffee, Mary.

(c) <u>Don't talk</u> to me.... <u>Find</u> a new boyfriend.

(d) <u>Don't throw</u> your litter on the street. <u>Pick</u> it <u>up</u>!

(e) <u>Go</u> straight down 8th Ave. and <u>turn</u> left at the bakery.

(f) <u>Watch out</u>!

Focus 2

The challenge of imperatives is knowing how to use them appropriately. Exercises 2, 3, 4, and 5 present different functions or "speech acts" realized through imperatives within the context of various relationships.

Exercise 2

Use	Picture #
A. giving advice	2
B. giving an order	5
C. giving a warning when there is danger	1
D. making a polite request	6
E. politely offering something	4
F. giving directions	3

Exercise 3

This exercise gets students to reflect on the real social function of this text.

Part A

Caution: <u>Keep away</u> from heat and flame. <u>Open</u> windows and doors when you paint. If you have headaches or feel dizzy, <u>get</u> more fresh air or <u>cover</u> your mouth and nose. If you feel sick, <u>leave</u> the room. <u>Close</u> the paint container after each use. <u>Avoid</u> contact with skin. <u>Do not swallow</u>. <u>Keep</u> out of the reach of children.

Part B

1. b.   2. c.

Exercise 4

Part A

1. Be
2. Look
3. Use
4. Obey
5. Leave (*or* Keep)
6. Wear
7. Don't drive
8. Don't drink
9. Use
10. Keep

Part B

1. b.   2. a.

Exercise 5

Another variation on this exercise would be to have the statements on the left and the responses on the right written on separate cards or slips of paper. Each student is given a card and is asked to memorize what is written. The students then walk around the room, saying their sentence and trying to find the appropriate match. When they find their match, they sit down together until all students have finished. Then, each pair can recite their statement and response.

PART A

1. d
2. j
3. a
4. h
5. b
6. c
7. f
8. e
9. i
10. g

PART B

1. a.

Exercise 6

These idiomatic expressions are very common and could generate much discussion. It would be a good idea for students to work in pairs or small groups so they can rely on each other's knowledge. After students have finished the exercise, you might ask them to think of a situation in which they would use that expression. For example, a situation in which one would use "Give me a break!" could possibly be a mother nagging her teenage son to do his homework, clean up his room, take out the garbage, etc., until he responds with that expression. Give one expression to a pair of students and have them come up with a situation. They could then either write a dialogue or do a role-play in front of the class.

Affirmative

1. _Give_ me a break!
2. _Be_ careful.
3. _Take_ it easy.
4. _Go_ ahead.
5. _Have_ a good day.
6. _Keep_ in touch.
7. _Leave_ me alone.
8. _Do_ the best you can.

Negative

1. _Don't rock_ the boat.
2. _Don't talk_ to strangers.
3. _Don't cry_ over spilled milk.
4. _Don't drink_ and drive.

Focus 3

Students will often use imperatives inappropriately because of prior teaching that concentrated strictly on form. This is why they also need to consider appropriateness — when, and with whom, imperatives can be used.

Exercise 7

These situations could involve a great deal of discussion, especially of cultural differences.

1. Yes
2. No
3. Yes
4. No
5. No
6. Yes
7. It depends. In this situation, it is understood that it is an emergency and the driver probably wouldn't be offended.
8. In general, this would be considered really rude.
9. Yes

Activities

Activity 1

Students are asked to collect public or household notices. These can include instructions for any electronic device or other apparatus — walkman, food processor, vacuum cleaner, recycling notices, etc. Only one example has been included here, but there are many to be found everywhere. Help students understand the concepts or cultural aspects of these notices, as in the one on protecting your belongings from thieves at the public library.

Have students post their notices around the room and create a "poster session" in which students can talk about their notice to groups that pass by. Students can identify the imperatives in each notice.

Activity 2

Bring in magazines so that students can cut out pictures to create their pamphlets. Display the different pamphlets after students have finished.

Activity 3

This text is an excerpt from a real student's journal entry. Make it clear to students that the purpose of the activity is not to correct the student's grammar, but to offer him a viable, acceptable solution. They could write a letter of advice to the student in question. Have students work in groups, giving advice to this frustrated student of English. Ask them to write their advice on butcher block paper so that each group can post their advice on the board and talk about their ideas. You can also check the imperatives to see if they are correct. We urge you to try to extract similar texts from your own students' journals. It is very powerful when students can actually respond to each other's real problems.

Activity 4

This activity could stimulate an interesting exchange of cultural information. You could have students sit in culturally homogeneous groups to generate imperatives about their particular culture; or you could mix cultures so that students could come up with ideas by making comparisons. You might want to present some general categories to the class such as restaurants, clothing/dress codes, holidays and customs, dating, tipping, etc., in order to help students focus.

UNIT 14

Prepositions of Direction

Task

Allow students some time to become familiar with the map presented in the task. Have them work in groups to follow Sandy and Charlie's routes, and then have each group compare their answers. The answers to the task may vary. Possible answers include:

Where does Sandy go on Saturday night?   { *She goes to the disco.* / *to a disco.* }

What does she do there?   *She probably dances.*

Where does Charlie go on Saturday night?   *He goes to the post office.*

What does he do there?   { *He works the night shift.* / *there.* }

Focus 1

Have students review prepositions of location first and then introduce prepositions of direction. You could adopt an inductive approach by showing students sentences with both prepositions of location and prepositions of direction, and asking them to figure out that prepositions of direction are used with verbs of movement.

Exercise 1

A. Sandy <u>walks</u> (out of) her house and <u>goes</u> (to) the corner. She <u>gets</u> (on) the #7 bus. She <u>gets</u> (off) the bus at Church Avenue and 5th Street. She <u>walks</u> (down) 5th Street to Tower Avenue. She <u>walks</u> (across) Tower Avenue and <u>goes</u> (into) the building on the corner of 5th and Tower. She takes the elevator (up to) the 5th floor. She leaves there at 3:00 A.M.

58

B. At 10:00 P.M., Charlie gets (into) his car and drives (down) Tower Avenue. He usually drives (past) the coffee shop between 2nd and 3rd Streets, but sometimes he stops and buys a cup of coffee. He turns right on 2nd Street and makes another right on Clinton Avenue. He drives (past) the tower and (into) the parking lot on the corner of 3rd Street. He gets (out of) his car, walks (across) the parking lot, and (into) the building. He leaves there at 6:00 A.M.

Focus 2

The prepositions of direction in this unit are presented in groups or "chunks" so students can learn them more easily.

Exercise 2

1. out of
2. on (to)
3. to
4. off (of)
5. away from
6. into

Exercise 3

1. across
2. through
3. over/across
4. up
5. around
6. down
7. past
8. along/down/up

Exercise 4

(1) into (2) to (3) on (to), or in (to) (4) to (5) to/past (6) over/across (7) along (8) into (9) out of (10) through (11) out of (12) to/past (13) out of (14) off (of), or out of

Focus 4

Involving students in activities where they are giving directions is an effective way to have them practice prepositions of direction. Use authentic local maps and have students give directions from their home to school, to each other's houses, to the shopping district, etc.

Exercise 5

1. At the bookstore
2. At Sal's Pizzeria (In Sal's Pizzeria)
3. At the Garage

Exercise 6

Answers may vary.

Exercise 7

This exercise offers a nonverbal way of checking whether or not students really understand the prepositions of direction. Students mime one of the two commands.

Exercise 8

1. through
2. off/out of/into
3. across/into
4. (a) into   (b) out of
5. away from
6. (a) to   (b) along/on   (c) under   (d) off (of)   (e) into

Activities

Activity 1

If possible, have students tape-record their routes and work in pairs to transcribe the tape on butcher block paper. You can then ask them to work with the grammar by circling the prepositions of direction, underlining the prepositions of location, etc.

Activity 2

After students have compiled a number of cards, this can be used as a warm-up activity at the start of another class. You could also change it into a game in which students get points for creating new and interesting commands.

Activity 4

Allow students enough time to prepare this treasure hunt. They could get really creative and venture out of the classroom. The students who go on the hunt can then come back and relate their experiences, using the prepositions of direction in sentences.

UNIT 15

Direct Objects and Object Pronouns

Task

Have students discuss the picture sequence and elaborate the story before reading. Focus on interpreting the doctor's gestures in Pictures 4 and 5. Elicit relevant vocabulary items. You may want to use the two comprehension questions as pre-reading questions to be answered by studying the cartoons and later confirmed by reading. Write the vocabulary that students generate on the board and then have them read the story.

1. b.   2. c.

Exercise 1

1. Pom Pom Perry plays (the guitar).
2. He loves (his job).
3. He sees (spots) before his eyes.
4. Finally, one day he visits (his eye doctor).
5. The doctor examines (Perry).
6. He tests (Perry's vision).
7. Perry reads (the chart).
8. The doctor doesn't understand (the problem).
9. The doctor never sees (Perry's hat).
10. Perry takes (his hat and his guitar) and goes home.

Exercise 2

1. (a) I   (b) them
2. (a) I   (b) them   (c) I   (d) them
3. (a) I   (b) I   (c) them
4. (a) I   (b) it
5. (a) I   (b) her
6. (a) She   (b) them   (c) She   (d) me
7. (a) I   (b) it   (c) It   (d) me   (e) them   (f) me   (g) me   (h) I

61

Exercise 4

Ted loves his girlfriend Alice. He also likes Maggie. Alice doesn't know about <u>her</u>. Maggie works with Ted. She sees <u>him</u> every day. He sometimes invites <u>her</u> to dinner. He likes to talk with <u>her</u>. He doesn't love Maggie, but she loves <u>him</u>. She thinks about <u>him</u> all the time. Ted doesn't want to leave Alice. He can't tell <u>her</u> about Maggie. Ted cares for both Alice and Maggie. He doesn't know what to do. He doesn't want to hurt <u>them</u>. He says to himself, "What's the matter with me? Alice loves <u>me</u> and I love <u>her</u>. I must end my relationship with Maggie!"

Focus 3

Explain anaphoric reference to students by showing how object pronouns refer to noun phrases in an earlier part of the text. When doing reading or writing activities with your students, ask them to point out object pronouns and say what they are referring to.

Exercise 5

"I don't understand (these spots). I am really worried about <u>them</u> now. It's strange. Sometimes I see <u>them</u> and sometimes I don't see <u>them</u>. (My eyes) are fine. The doctor checked <u>them</u>. (My vision) is good. The doctor tested <u>it</u>. (The doctor)'s a good doctor. I can't be angry at <u>him</u>. Maybe it's (my hat). When I wear <u>it</u>, I see (the spots). When I don't wear <u>it</u>, I don't see <u>them</u>. That's it! It's my hat! I'm allergic to my hat! I must discuss this with (the doctor). I'll call <u>him</u> tomorrow."

Exercise 6

1. (a) me   (b) you
2. (a) her
3. (a) her   (b) her   (c) you
4. (a) us   (b) her   (c) me   (d) you
5. (a) her   (b) me

Exercise 7

After students have finished asking their partners the questions, you could have them choose one interesting item they learned about their partner to report to the class. Answers may vary.

Questions	Answers (pronouns)
1. How often do you call your parents?	*them*
2. How often do you do your laundry?	*it*
3. How often do you visit the dentist?	*him/her*
4. How often do you wash your car?	*it*
5. How often do you read the newspaper?	*it*
6. How often do you brush your teeth?	*them*
7. How often do you wash your hair?	*it*
8. How often do you see your friends?	*them*
9. How often do you drink coffee?	*it*
10. How often do you do the shopping?	*it*

Activities

Activity 2

It might be useful to have a picture chart of different occupations to help students write sentences.

Activity 3

If students have trouble working alone on this, have the entire class generate personal habits and write them on the board. Students could then choose from the list and read the statement to the class.

Activity 4

Add items that may be fun to use in this activity, such as ice cream ("Children love it."), airplanes ("Airlines own them." "Pilots fly them."), pets, etc.

UNIT 16

Can versus Know How To; And/But

Task

Ensure that students understand the word *versatile* here.
Answers to task:

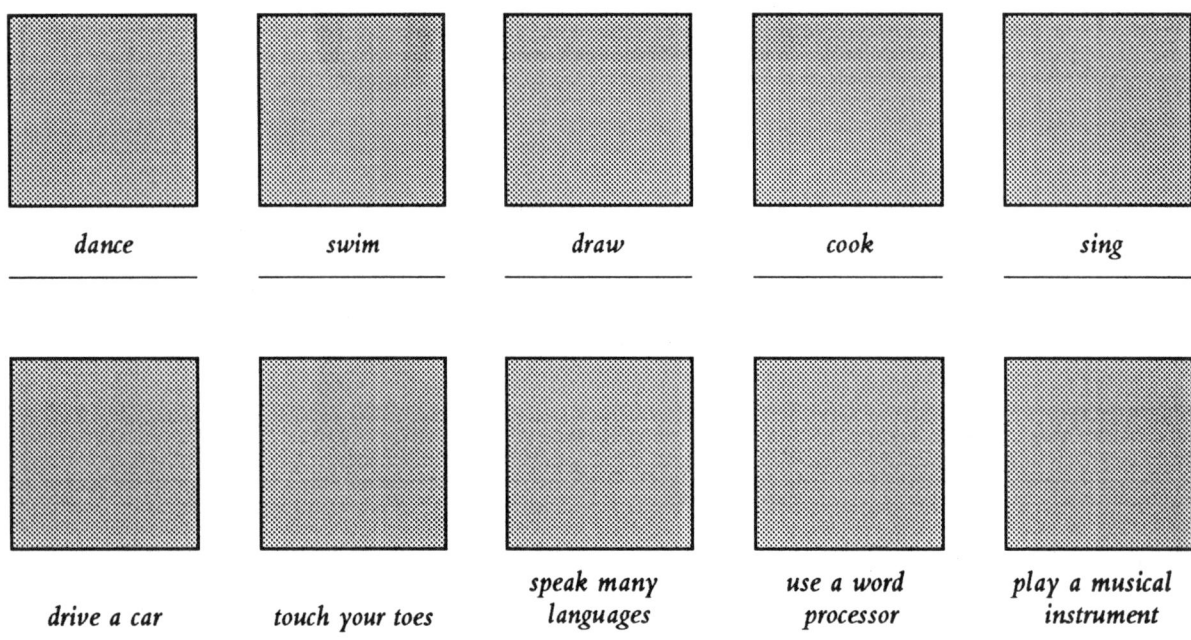

dance swim draw cook sing

drive a car touch your toes speak many languages use a word processor play a musical instrument

Focus 1

This is the first time in the text that the term *modal verb* is used. Although you may not think it is so important for students to learn grammar terminology, it is useful for them to hear the term *modal* both in preparation for *will* in Unit 23 and for the other modals introduced in later books in this series. The category *modal* automatically provides information about form.

Exercise 1

Answers may vary.

Exercise 2

1. He can't hear his mother.
2. She can swim.
3. They can eat with chopsticks.
4. She can't open the jar.
5. He can't walk.
6. He can't go to work.
7. They can't see the screen.
8. They can speak English.

Exercise 3

The self-assessment grid in this exercise contains all of the "speech acts" that have been presented in Use Boxes up to this point in the book. In doing this exercise, students review what they have learned and how well they've learned it. If there are any problems in the execution of these speech acts, refer students back to the Focus Boxes in the units dealing with each speech act. You might want to create some role-play situations to check the interactive skills of the students who answer YES, and to reinforce the skills of those who answer NO.

Focus 2

Learners will tend to use *do/does* along with *can* in questions. Reinforce the use of modal verbs as auxiliary (helping) verbs.

Exercise 4

Having students ask yes/no questions about what men and women **can** do should involve students in lively discussion. Remember, the focus is on the meaning having to do with "ability." You may need to review some of the professions and the skills involved in each before doing this exercise. To vary the exercise, put a sign saying *Women* on one side of the room, another sign saying *Men* on the other side of the room, and a third sign saying *Both* on a third wall. Then ask a question such as, "Can women or men be good combat soldiers?" Have students walk to the sign representing the position with which they agree.

Answers to these questions may vary.

1. Can a woman work as a fire fighter?
2. Can women be good combat soldiers?
3. Can a man be a good nurse?
4. Can men teach kindergarten?
5. Can women be mounted police officers?
6. Can a woman be a construction worker?
7. Can a man work as a housekeeper?
8. Can a woman be President of a country?

Exercise 5

Answers may vary. Encourage students to make additional statements with *can/can't* to justify their opinions.

Exercise 6

This Exercise will also provoke some discussion. Answers to questions may vary.

1. Can people live without food for six months?
2. Can a computer think?
3. Can smoking cause cancer?
4. Can an airplane fly from New York to Paris in four hours?
5. Can a person run twenty-five miles an hour?
6. Can a river flow uphill?
7. Can we communicate with people on other planets?
8. Can a person learn a language in a week?
9. Can cars run on alcohol?
10. Can you think of any more questions?

Focus 3

This Focus Box distinguishes between learned ability and natural ability, using *can* and *know how to*. Have students generate other examples where they can use either *can* or *know how to*, or just *can*. You might use pictures as cues to do this. Reinforce the use of *do/does* with *know how to* as opposed to *can*.

Exercise 7

Ask students to explain why they can't use *know how to* in some cases, as in #1.

1. A blind person can't see. *(Natural Ability)*

2. A dog can live for twenty-five years. *(Natural Ability)*

3. Infants can't walk. *(Learned Ability)*
   Infants don't know how to walk.

4. A deaf person can't hear. *(Natural Ability)*

5. Fish can't breathe on land. *(Natural Ability)*

6. Mechanics can fix cars. *(Learned ability)*
   Mechanics know how to fix cars.

7. Men can take care of babies. *(Learned Ability)*
   Men know how to take care of babies.

8. A man can't have a baby. *(Natural Ability)*

9. Doctors can cure some diseases. *(Learned ability)*
   Doctors know how to cure some diseases.

Exercise 8

Answers may vary. For example:

1. I can type and I can use a word processor.
   I can type, but I can't use a word processor.

Focus 5

There are two Communication Strategies presented in this Focus Box. The first is simply a means of checking the accuracy of one's language. The second is a means of compensating for what one doesn't know how to say in English. The aim here is to teach students how to use gestures and miming to get their meaning across and learn more language at the same time. We also suggest teaching circumlocution strategies here; that is, teaching students how to keep talking until the listener can grasp their meaning and offer help. If students are regularly encouraged to use these compensation strategies, they will be better communicators and better learners, taking more risks and dropping out of conversations less readily.

Exercise 9

Students mime the action in order to practice communication strategies presented in Focus 5. For example, one student mimes the action of skiing while asking, "How can I say _____ in English?"

Activities

Activity 2

An extension of this activity is to bring in real job advertisements from the classifieds to familiarize students with ads. Try to find ads that would be suitable to your student population. Or you can ask students to look at the classifieds and cut out ads that appeal to them. They could then write questions and role-play job interviews.

Activity 4

This activity could provoke a lot of discussion. You might want to tape-record the discussion and transcribe it to correct the language that is generated.

Activity 5

This activity can be varied by doing it as a bingo game. Add a few more boxes to the grid to create either sixteen or twenty-five squares. Each student has a grid and walks around the room asking yes/no questions with *can*. If a respondent says YES, the student writes that person's name in the square and then goes on to the next person. If the respondent says NO, another question is asked until the person says YES. This procedure is repeated until someone wins. To win, the student must have completed a row of different names either vertically, horizontally, or diagonally.

UNIT 17

Adverbs of Manner

Task

Make sure students are familiar with the vocabulary in the task before checking the columns.

1. No
2. No
3. No
4. Yes
5. I don't know.
6. Yes
7. Yes
8. Yes
9. I don't know.
10. Yes

Exercise 1

1. Bill is a <u>careful</u> driver.
2. He eats (moderately).
3. He drives (slowly).
4. He's a <u>heavy</u> drinker.
5. He works (hard).
6. He drives (carelessly).
7. He is a <u>big</u> eater.
8. He drives (fast).
9. He dresses (neatly).
10. He is a <u>heavy</u> smoker.

Exercise 2

1. Baryshnikov dances gracefully.
2. Ben Johnson runs fast.
3. My father smokes heavily.
4. The President speaks well.
5. Pavarotti sings wonderfully.

6. Teachers work hard.
7. Our teacher speaks clearly.
8. Some children learn slowly.
9. These painters work sloppily.
10. She reads quickly.

Exercise 3

1. Performer
2. Activity
3. Activity
4. Performer
5. Performer
6. Activity
7. Performer
8. Activity

Exercise 4

This is a challenging and fun exercise students can do in pairs.

1. happily
2. sadly
3. quickly
4. incorrectly
5. politely
6. impolitely
7. angrily
8. nervously
9. shyly
10. kindly

Exercise 5

Another way of doing this exercise as a listening activity is to have five students read the clues aloud. The class only sees the occupations and then must assign an occupation to the appropriate student.

1. C. Teacher
2. E. Emergency Medical Technician or Paramedic
3. A. Secretary for the U.N.
4. D. Artist
5. B. Lawyer

Exercise 6

1. (a) She speaks slowly.
   (b) She pronounces words clearly.
   (c) She prepares carefully.
2. (d) She types fast.
   (e) She answers the phone politely.
   (f) She takes messages accurately.
3. (g) He drives slowly.
   (h) He responds quickly.

4. **(i)** She sings well.

   (j) She dances fantastically.

5. **(k)** She studies hard.

   (l) She guesses intelligently.

   (m) She asks questions constantly.

Exercise 7

Answers may vary. Possible answers include:

1. He's a heavy smoker.   He smokes heavily.
2. She's a great cook.   She cooks well.
3. She's a hard worker.   She works hard.
4. He's a fast driver.   He drives fast.
5. He's a good/great performer.   He performs well.

Exercise 8

Answers may vary. Possible answers include:

1. He drives very slowly.
2. He speaks very fast.   He doesn't speak very clearly.
3. She cooks very well.
4. He works very hard.
5. She types very fast.

Activities

Activity 1

Another way of doing this activity is to have about twenty adverbs written on index cards for each student in a group to pick out. The groups then tell the student to do something "in that manner," and the student mimes the action. By having the cards already set up, you can offer interesting adverbs for students to mime.

Activity 3

After students write their paragraphs, have them sit in a circle and share their writing with the group. You might want to take notes on mistakes they make and then work on correction.

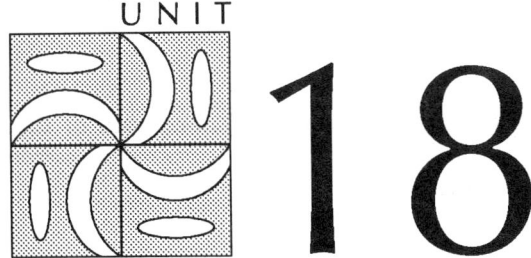

Present Progressive Tense

The present progressive is often introduced before the simple present tense because it is relatively easy to form once the verb *be* has been acquired, and because its meaning is tangible and therefore easy to demonstrate. However, the present progressive is introduced well after the simple present tense in this book in order to avoid overgeneralization.

Task

This unit deals with the roles of men and women in modern American society. The task is written to show the opposition between the simple present, expressing habits and routines, and the present progressive, expressing the ongoing and temporary nature of an activity. Have students work in groups. Elicit vocabulary and expressions from students and write them on the board to facilitate the task.

Exercise 1

...But today, Robin (is attending) a meeting at the college, so Regis (is staying) home and (taking) care of the children. It is 7:30 P.M. and Robin (is walking) through the door right now....

Robin: Hello dear. Is everything under control here?

Regis: ...under control? (Are) you (kidding)! Everything ('s going) wrong here....

1. The food ('s burning) in the oven.
2. The pots (are boiling) over on the stove.
3. Suzy ('s lying) in front of the television, hypnotized.
4. The television (is blasting), and it ('s giving) me a terrible headache!
5. Frankie and the dog (are fighting) over a stuffed animal.
6. Frankie (is crying).
7. The dog ('s barking).
8. Jimmy ('s playing) cowboy on my back.
9. His cowboy boots (are hurting) my stomach!
10. The phone ('s ringing). I ('m going) crazy here! Help!

Focus 2

You might try working inductively. Present various sentences to your students and have them come up with the spelling rules.

Exercise 2

1. is screaming
2. is making
3. is biting
4. is growling
5. is sitting
6. is worrying
7. is choking
8. is getting
9. is beginning
10. is smiling
11. are killing
12. is dying

Exercise 3

1. Robin isn't / Robin's not } taking care of the children today.
2. Robin isn't / Robin's not } preparing dinner tonight.
3. Robin isn't / Robin's not } staying home today.
4. Regis isn't / Regis's not } having a good day today.
5. The children aren't / The children're not } listening to Regis.
6. Suzy isn't / Suzy's not } helping Regis.
7. Regis isn't / Regis's not } answering the phone.
8. Regis isn't / Regis's not } paying attention to the dinner in the oven.
9. Regis isn't / Regis's not } smiling.
10. Regis isn't / Regis's not } enjoying fatherhood today.

Exercise 4

1. Mrs. Bainbridge is having a party at her house this evening.
2. The guests are talking in the living room.
3. Mr. and Mrs. Desmond aren't talking to the other guests.
4. Mr. and Mrs. Desmond are feeling very bored right now.
5. Mr. and Mrs. Desmond aren't enjoying the party.
6. Mr. and Mrs. Desmond aren't leaving by the front door.
7. Mr. and Mrs. Desmond are climbing out the window at the moment.
8. Mr. and Mrs. Desmond are trying to escape.
9. Mr. Desmond is holding his hat between his teeth.
10. Mrs. Desmond is helping Mr. Desmond climb out the window.

Exercise 5

These statements reflect changes in the American family life-style. You may want to have students make statements about male/female roles in their own countries as well.

Answers may vary. One example:

1. Women are getting good jobs nowadays.
   These days, women are getting good jobs.

Exercise 6

Answers may vary. Possible answers include:

Simple Present	Present Progressive
	A. Today, Robin isn't taking care of the children. Today, Robin is attending a meeting. Today, Regis is taking care of the children.
2. Robin usually cooks dinner in the evening.	
	C. The children aren't behaving at home. The children are driving their father crazy.
4. Suzy usually doesn't watch TV. She usually does her homework.	
	E. Tonight, Robin isn't cooking dinner. Regis is cooking tonight.

Exercise 7

Answers may vary. Some examples are:

1. I do my homework every day, but I'm not doing homework right now.
2. I usually write letters home once a week, but I'm not writing a letter at the moment.

Exercise 8

After students have completed the exercise, have them role-play the dialogues.

1. (a) need   (b) am watching
2. (a) doing   (b) am/'m   (c) am/'m trying   (d) is attending
3. (a) is pulling   (b) am/'m talking   (c) know   (d) comes   (e) are doing
4. (a) is   (b) am/'m coming   (c) is/'s happening   (d) are behaving   (e) are/'re behaving   (f) talk

Exercise 9

Since students number the pictures in any order from 1 to 12, this exercise can be repeated if students need more practice. This also forces students to listen to what their partners are saying in order to sequence the pictures. Give students additional adjectives or verbs to use when doing this exercise. For example, in Picture A the girl seems sad or depressed. Answers may vary. Possible answers include:

	Stative Verb	Present Progressive
Picture A:	She looks/seems sad/upset.	She's crying.
Picture B:	He looks happy.	He's smiling.
Picture C:	He looks tired.	He's yawning.
Picture D:	He looks angry/tense.	He's snarling./He's clenching his fists.
Picture E:	He seems nervous.	He's smoking frantically.

Picture F:	She looks surprised.	She's opening up a present./She's looking at a diamond ring./She's opening up a little box with a diamond ring in it.
Picture G:	He looks sick.	He's holding his head and stomach.
Picture H:	She looks bored.	She's staring out the window.
Picture I:	She looks confused.	She's deciding about detergents./She's trying to choose a detergent.
Picture J:	He seems scared.	He's watching a horror movie.
Picture K:	He looks hot.	He's sweating.
Picture L:	He looks cold.	He's shivering.

Exercise 10

1. Are the children helping their father?
2. Are Frankie and the dog fighting?
3. Are the pots boiling over?
4. Is their dinner burning?
5. Is Regis losing his patience?
6. Is Jimmy hurting his father?
7. Is the dog biting the stuffed animal?
8. Is Robin walking through the door?
9. Is Robin smiling?
10. Are men and women taking care of their children together nowadays?

Exercise 11

1. Why are Frankie and the dog fighting?
2. Who(m) is Robin meeting today?
3. What is Robin thinking?
4. Why are they eating peanut butter and jelly sandwiches for dinner?
5. Who is watching the children today?
6. Why is Regis taking two aspirins?
7. Where is Robin's meeting taking place?
8. Who is walking through the door right now?
9. How are the children behaving?
10. How is Regis feeling right now?
11. Who is making a lot of noise?

Exercise 12

1. Frankie and the dog are fighting.
2. He has a new TV.
3. The TV is blasting.
4. Why are you working today?
5. Do you need any help?
6. What is Robin thinking?
7. Does she believe him?
8. Right now, he is playing cowboy on his father's back.
9. The soup smells bad.
10. Where are you going?

Activities

Activity 1

As students are writing their sentences, you can have two students writing on the blackboard or on transparencies, which you can then use to work on correction.

Students may have trouble with the specialized vocabulary, so elicit the vocabulary in the picture before they write their sentences.

Things Wrong in the Picture:

1. Regis is wearing one shoe.
2. Robin is diving into a sand box and not a swimming pool.
3. Suzy is reading a book upside down.
4. Frankie is lifting heavy weights/a barbell.
5. The dog is digging a hole with a shovel.
6. A bear is sunbathing on a lounge chair.
7. Jimmy is playing tennis with a baseball bat.
8. The fish are flying in the air.
9. The squirrels are speaking French.
10. Bananas and apples are growing on the tree.

As a follow-up to this activity, you can ask students to draw a picture in which there are several things going wrong. Use it for a subsequent lesson.

Past Tense of *Be*

Task

While piloting the material for this book with students of many nationalities, we found that the story of "Cinderella" seemed to be universal; thus, familiar to everyone. This task, then, is partly based on the learners' background knowledge. However, any students who may not be familiar with "Cinderella" can also derive clues from the pictures and from the text itself. The picture-labeling activity should be carefully checked, especially those pictures illustrating more than one lexical item. The text is written so that it loses coherence if the learner makes an incorrect choice. These three types of clues — the learner's background knowledge, the pictures, and the coherence of the written text — should allow learners to complete the task successfully.

Part A

A. Palace Glass steps slipper
   <u>Palace</u> <u>steps</u> <u>slipper</u>

B. The <u>Duke</u>

C. <u>Cinderella</u>

D. Step-<u>sisters</u> <u>Invitation</u> Step-<u>mother</u>

E. Magic <u>wand</u> Fairy <u>godmother</u>

F. <u>Prince</u> <u>The Ball</u>

Part B

1. poor and beautiful
2. mean
3. spoiled and ugly
4. an invitation to the Prince's ball in the mail
5. handsome and charming
6. with her stepsisters
7. was not ready
8. magic wand
9. on the palace steps
10. "Whose foot was in this tiny glass slipper last night?"
11. Cinderella's
12. Cinderella

Focus 1

We have also included *There + Be* in the simple past in this Focus Box, since students have already been introduced to *there* (Unit 10). You may want to review Focus Box 1 on page 106, which explains that *there* is used for describing and showing the existence or location of something that represents new information.

Exercise 1

1. was
2. was
3. was
4. were
5. were
6. was
7. was
8. were
9. were

Exercise 2

1. were
2. was
3. was
4. were
5. were
6. was
7. were
8. was
9. were
10. was
11. was

Exercise 3

1. She wasn't rich and/or ugly. / She was poor and beautiful.
2. Her stepmother wasn't kind. / She was mean.
3. Her stepsisters weren't sweet and/or pretty. / They were mean and ugly.
4. The Prince wasn't ugly and/or nasty. / He was handsome and kind.
5. The glass slipper wasn't the stepmother's. / It was Cinderella's.
6. The Prince wasn't in love with Cinderella's stepsister. / He was in love with Cinderella.
7. There was no ball at Cinderella's house. / There was a ball at the palace.
8. There weren't two princes at the ball. / There was one prince.

Exercise 4

Alice: was
Carol: was
Michael: wasn't / was
Carol: were
Michael: was
Carol: wasn't/was not *(for emphasis)* / was
Michael: wasn't
Carol: was
Michael: weren't
Carol: were
Michael: were
Carol: weren't/were not *(for emphasis)* / were / weren't

Exercise 5

This exercise offers a modern-day version of the "Cinderella" story. You might want to talk about psychologists or therapists, since this might be a new concept to certain students.

(1) was
(2) were
(3) was
(4) was
(5) was
(6) wasn't
(7) wasn't
(8) were
(9) wasn't
(10) were
(11) were
(12) was
(13) was
(14) was
(15) was
(16) was
(17) wasn't
(18) were
(19) were
(20) was
(21) was
(22) were
(23) was
(24) was
(25) was
(26) was
(27) wasn't
(28) was
(29) was
(30) was
(31) was
(32) were

Exercise 6

These questions might provoke some interesting discussion. Have students share this information with the whole class. Concentrate on question 5 in preparation for Activity 3, in which students are asked to "set the state" or write beginnings of stories.

1. Was Cinderella lucky?
2. Was the stepmother happy at the end of the story?
3. Was the end of the story fair?
4. Was the story "Cinderella" important to you when you were a child?
5. Were fairy tales popular when you were a child?

Exercise 7

You might want to bring in some photographs of these famous personalities to help students do this exercise. Have them work in groups so they can rely on each other's background knowledge.

Answers may vary. Possible answers include:

1. Was Marilyn Monroe a famous American actress?
   Yes, she was.
2. Were the Marx Brothers well-known German Communists?
   No, they weren't. They were American actors and comedians.
3. Was Mao a political leader in The People's Republic of China?
   Yes, he was.
4. Were the Beatles famous hairdressers in the 1960s?
   No, they weren't. They were musicians in the 1960s.
5. Was John Kennedy President of the United States in the 1960s?
   Yes, he was.
6. Was Martin Luther King a well-known African leader?
   No, he wasn't. He was a well-known African-American leader.
7. Was Nelson Mandela a prisoner in South Africa?
   Yes, he was.

Exercise 8

Furlock:	Was there
Police Officer:	there was
Furlock:	Were there
Police Officer:	there weren't
Furlock:	Was there
Furlock:	Were there
Police Officer:	There was

Exercise 9

Answers may vary. Possible answers include:

1. **Cinderella:** It was in your closet <u>this morning/last night/yesterday</u>.
   Stepsister: I know it was in my closet [<u>same as above</u>], but it isn't there <u>now</u>.
2. **Cinderella:** They were under your bed [<u>use any past time expression</u>].
   Stepsister: Well, they aren't there [<u>use present time expression</u>].
3. **The Prince:** Where is that beautiful woman? She was at the palace <u>last night/yesterday</u>, but she isn't here <u>now/today</u>.
4. **Cinderella:** Where is that slipper? It was on my foot <u>last night</u>, but it isn't there <u>now</u>.

Exercise 10

Part A

Jim: <u>Where were you</u> yesterday afternoon, Joan?
Joan: What do you mean where was I yesterday afternoon? I <u>was</u> in class!
Jim: Oh no you <u>weren't</u>. I <u>was</u> in class and you <u>weren't</u> there.
Joan: OK, Jim. The truth is I <u>was</u> in the library.
Jim: In the library? <u>Why were you</u> in the library?
Joan: To study for a test.
Jim: <u>Who was</u> with you in the library?
Joan: Well, Larry <u>was</u> with me.
Jim: And <u>whose</u> idea was it to study together in the library?
Joan: It <u>was</u> Larry's idea, Jim.
Jim: And <u>how</u> was studying with Larry?
Joan: It <u>was</u> fine, Jim. Larry's smart. But don't worry, he's just a friend.

Part B

1. b.   2. a.

Exercise 11

1. Were her stepsisters beautiful?
2. Her stepsisters were mean.
3. Was Cinderella lucky?
4. Where was her glass slipper?
5. Why was the Prince in love with Cinderella?
6. Was the story "Cinderella" popular in your country?
7. There wasn't any shade at Disney World./
   There was no shade at Disney World.
8. There were no children at the ball./
   There weren't any children at the ball.

Activities

Activity 2

You may want to pick a time frame for students to do this activity such as "Where were you last weekend? last summer? five summers ago?" Before students do this activity, ask them to bring in pictures of the places they will be describing.

Activity 3

You can assign a specific genre to different groups. For example, one group writes a love story, another a horror story. Without saying what kind of story it is, the group reads their story aloud, and the class decides which genre it is. Because of the students' limitations (only the verb *be*), they can only be asked to set the scene; in other words, to create the beginning of a story, as in the examples.

UNIT 20 Past Tense

Task

This task works best if students are in groups, exchanging their hypotheses about the mystery. You might choose one person in the group to be the note-taker or recorder who, at the end of fifteen minutes, could present the group's hypotheses to the class. If students have not come up with a definitive answer after the task, you do not necessarily have to tell them the correct answer. They will get the solution in Exercise 5.

Focus 1

The specificity of regular past tense verbs: Spelling and pronunciation are dealt with first in this unit.

Exercise 1

REGULAR PAST TENSE VERBS:

> Many students thought Ms. Ditto was the best ESL teacher in the English Language Center. Three years ago, she began to use a VCR in her classes. She brought in videotapes every semester. She taught the students a lot. They <u>enjoyed</u> her classes and really <u>liked</u> her.
>
> Only one student, Harry, didn't like Ms. Ditto. Harry <u>hated</u> her because he <u>failed</u> her course twice. Last summer, he got a job in the language lab because he <u>needed</u> money to register for her class again this semester. Yes, Harry felt angry at Ms. Ditto.
>
> Two weeks ago, just before the new semester <u>started</u>, the Director of the English Language Center heard about budget cuts in the university. The university didn't have money to pay the teachers, so they didn't rehire Ms. Ditto. Everyone was sad, including the Director. Harry just <u>laughed</u>!
>
> Yesterday morning was the first day of the new semester. Professor Paul <u>wanted</u> to use the VCR. He <u>asked</u> Harry to open the language lab. But when Harry <u>opened</u> the door to the lab, the VCR was not there. In its place, there was a typewritten note with a signature on it. The note said:
>
> *Today, I very sad. I no can work in English Language Center because there no have money to pay me. What I can do now? How I can live? I take this VCR because I have angry. Please understand my. I sorry...*
>
> *Miss Ditto*
>
> Harry immediately <u>reported</u> the robbery to the Director, and gave her the note.

Exercise 2

1. enjoyed
2. used
3. helped
4. studied
5. learned
6. discussed
7. registered
8. liked
9. stopped
10. cried
11. occurred
12. disappeared

Focus 2

The pronunciation of the *-ed* ending in the regular past tense is challenging to students and needs to be addressed from the start.

Exercise 3

You could have students discuss what is going on in each of the pictures of the Bookworm Benny cartoons before they read the story. Or you could follow the directions, have them read the story first, and then reorder the pictures. Have students work in pairs to determine the pronunciation of each verb.

	t	d	Id
1. liked	×		
2. worked	×		
3. finished	×		
4. called		×	
5. answered		×	
6. remembered		×	
7. talked	×		
8. hated			×
9. decided			×
10. rolled		×	
11. waited			×
12. landed			×
13. yelled		×	
14. asked	×		
15. pointed			×
16. trusted			×
17. punished	×		

Exercise 4

Another way of doing this exercise is to have students tape-record their stories first and then transcribe them as a group on large (newsprint) paper. You could then work on correcting the stories and having them re-tape the corrected versions.

Exercise 5

This exercise provides the solution to the mystery, in case of any remaining ambiguity.

(1) learned   (2) believed   (3) suspected   (4) locked   (5) remembered   (6) looked   (7) noticed   (8) asked   (9) discussed   (10) confessed

Focus 3

This Focus Box deals with the specificity of irregular past tense verbs: their various forms. The categorization should help learners remember the forms. If possible, have students write the forms on butcher block paper and keep the lists up around the room.

Exercise 6

IRREGULAR PAST TENSE VERBS:

Many students <u>thought</u> Ms. Ditto <u>was</u> the best ESL teacher in the English Language Center. Three years ago, she <u>began</u> to use a VCR in her classes. She <u>brought</u> in videotapes every semester. She <u>taught</u> the students a lot. They enjoyed her classes and really liked her.

Only one student, Harry, didn't like Ms. Ditto. Harry hated her because he failed her course twice. Last summer, he <u>got</u> a job in the language lab because he needed money to register for her class again this semester. Yes, Harry <u>felt</u> angry at Ms. Ditto.

Two weeks ago, just before the new semester started, the Director of the English Language Center <u>heard</u> about budget cuts in the university. The university didn't have money to pay the teachers, so they didn't rehire Ms. Ditto. Everyone was sad, including the Director. Harry just laughed!

Yesterday morning was the first day of the new semester. Professor Paul wanted to use the VCR. He asked Harry to open the language lab. But when Harry opened the door to the lab, the VCR was not there. In its place, there was a typewritten note with a signature on it. The note <u>said</u>:

Today, I very sad. I no can work in English Language Center because there no have money to pay me. What I can do now? How I can live? I take this VCR because I have angry. Please understand my. I sorry...

Miss Ditto

Harry immediately reported the robbery to the Director, and <u>gave</u> her the note.

Exercise 7

1. flew
2. found
3. ate
4. went
5. took
6. stood
7. spent
8. bought
9. saw
10. met
11. spoke
12. thought

Exercise 8

1. sat
2. lost
3. went
4. got/broke
5. paid/drove
6. left/got
7. threw/stole
8. bought
9. went
10. fell
11. hurt
12. broke
13. caught
14. drank
15. left

Focus 4

Beginning with Focus 4, the past tense rules are the same and are thus presented as a common trunk.

Exercise 9

1. Last
2. ago
3. On/Last
4. On/Last
5. ago
6. yesterday
7. on
8. Yesterday

Exercise 10

To vary this exercise, write the time expressions on separate index cards and create a set of these for each group of 4–5 people. The students in the group take turns turning over an index card and making a statement using the past tense. Another twist could be to have students make either true or false statements, and then have the group decide whether the student is telling the truth or not.

Exercise 11

1. The other students didn't like Bookworm Benny.
2. The teacher trusted Benny.

3. The students tried to get Benny into trouble.
4. The students' plan for Benny didn't succeed.
5. Lisa and Kate didn't lose their luggage.
6. Lisa's camera didn't break.
7. Lisa and Kate spoke English in New York.
8. Lisa and Kate didn't get stuck on the subway.
9. Harry didn't notice the grammar mistakes in his note.
10. Ms. Ditto didn't sign the note.
11. Harry stole the VCR.
12. The Director didn't suspect Ms. Ditto.
13. Monique and Daniel didn't spend an evening in a jazz club.
14. Monique and Daniel didn't visit the United Nations.
15. Monique and Daniel didn't enjoy their vacation in New York.

Exercise 12

1. Did you like the Ms. Ditto story?
2. Did you enjoy being a detective?
3. Did you think Ms. Ditto was guilty?
4. Did you guess that Harry was the thief?
5. Did you find the grammar mistakes in Harry's note?
6. Did you correct the mistakes in the note?
7. Did you feel sorry for Harry?
8. Did you want to give Harry any advice?

Exercise 13

Students can generate their predictions orally or in writing. You could have students write their different versions of the ending on newsprint and post them around the room for all students to read. Students could then choose the best ending. The real ending can be found on page 238, at the end of the unit. You might want to look at the conclusion after students have completed this exercise, to compare endings. Or you might want to wait until Activity 1, in which students are asked to write endings for the story.

1. Did Jerry's cruise ship sink?
2. Did Jerry know how to swim?
3. Did Jerry die?
4. Did he find an island?
5. Did he have enough food?
6. Did he make tools?
7. Did he build a boat?
8. Did Jerry's luck get better?
9. Did the story have a happy ending?
10. Did Jerry find his way back home?

Exercise 14

1. Where did Jerry go?
   He went on a cruise.
2. Why did Jerry's ship sink?
   Jerry's ship sank because it ran into a bad storm.
3. What did Jerry do after the ship sank?
   He swam to a small island.
4. What did Jerry find on the island?
   He found fruit, fish, rocks, and trees.
5. What did Jerry eat there?
   He ate the fruit and fish.
6. How did Jerry build the boat?
   He built it from trees.
7. What did Jerry put on the boat?
   He put fresh fish and fruit on the boat.
8. How did Jerry feel?
   He felt great/hopeful.
9. How did the story end?

   Oral answers may range from one sentence to a complete ending here. This will depend on how creative the students are and how involved they become in Jerry's story. Any discussion at this point will enhance the students' ability to write their own endings when they get to Activity 1. The end of the story can be found on page 238, but try not to use this until students have generated and written their own endings.

Exercise 15

1. Who went to New York with Kate?
2. With whom did Lisa and Kate have lunch?/
   Whom (Who) did Lisa and Kate have lunch with?
3. For whom did they buy gifts?/
   Whom (Who) did they buy gifts for?
4. Who was the best ESL teacher in the English Language Center?
5. Who worked in the language lab?
6. Who typed the note?
7. Who signed the note?
8. To whom did Harry give the note?/
   Whom (Who) did Harry give the note to?
9. Whom (Who) did Harry hate?

Exercise 16

To facilitate this exchange of information, we have provided cues to indicate the type of question that must be formulated. You may want to do the first few examples with the entire class to show them how to do the exercise. Write the questions on the blackboard so students can see the correct questions.

TEXT A: **TEXT B:**

1. Where did Doina grow up?

2. Whom did she marry?

3. What did she do in 1976?

4. When did she have another daughter?

5. Why was Doina unhappy?

6. What did she think of?

7. What did she teach her children?

8. Where did she and her children swim?

9. Who caught them?

10. Where did Doina and her children go?

11. When did they make a second attempt to escape?

12. How did they leave Romania?

13. Where did they fly (to)?

14. Why did Doina go to school?

15. What did Doina write?

Exercise 17

1. This morning, I woke up early.
2. I saw him last night.
3. Harry wasn't sad.
4. They didn't meet the Mayor of New York City last week.
5. What did Harry want?
6. Harry didn't notice his mistakes.
7. Who signed the note?
8. What did the Director do?
9. What happened to Harry?
10. Where did Lisa and Kate go on vacation?
11. Who went with Lisa to New York?
12. How did Jerry build a boat?
13. They didn't have dinner in a Greek restaurant.
14. Whom did the Director suspect?

Activities

Activity 1

Again, students can exchange their endings and choose the best or most creative ending to the story.

Activity 2

This is a fun activity that can be played over and over again. As the teacher, you can first lead this activity by asking for the parts of speech ("Give me an adjective") and then writing them on the board. Then read the story to the class. Or you could let students take control of the activity, and do it as a whole class, in pairs, or in groups. If they work in pairs or groups, have each group read their version aloud. Decide which story is the funniest. Have students do other Mad Lib texts.

Activity 3

Ask students to bring in photographs from the vacation they are discussing.

Activity 4

This is a very interesting, interactive, and enjoyable activity that encourages students to work on question formation. As students come up with questions to ask the group, write the questions. These questions could be used later for error correction. In addition, students should justify their choices and explain why they thought #1, #2, or #3 was telling the truth.

UNIT 21

Indirect Objects with *To*

Task

Familiarize students with the different gifts in the task before they decide which gift they want to give each person. If you choose to have students work in groups, they can designate one student as the gift-giver and help that student match each gift to a person. (Note: Picture F represents a video game.)

Focus 1

This Focus Box differentiates between the meanings of direct and indirect objects.

Exercise 1

Answers may vary. Possible answers include:

A. I gave the camera to (my twenty-seven-year-old friend).

B. I gave the flowers to (my grandmother).

C. I gave the toaster to (the newlywed couple).

D. I gave the doll to (my friend's daughter).

E. I gave the earrings to (my mother).

F. I gave the video game to (my teenage nephew).

G. I gave the running shoes to (my single thirty-five-year-old friend).

H. I gave the compact disc player to (my girlfriend/boyfriend).

Focus 2

This Focus Box presents two possible sentence patterns using direct and indirect objects, without regard to use at this point.

Exercise 2

A. I gave my friend the camera.
B. I gave my grandmother the flowers.
C. I gave the newlywed couple the toaster.
D. I gave my friend's daughter the doll.
E. I gave my mother the earrings.
F. I gave my teenage nephew the video game.
G. I gave my single thirty-five-year-old friend the running shoes.
H. I gave my girlfriend/boyfriend the compact disc player.

Exercise 3

This exercise should generate some discussion about American customs as compared to customs in other countries. Such discussion would prepare students for Exercise 4 and Activity 3. If possible, bring in pictures and allow some time for students to ask other questions.

1. Friends give the mother flowers.
2. The father gives his friends cigars.
3. The couple sends their friends birth announcements.
4. The man gives his girlfriend a diamond ring.
5. Friends give the woman household gifts at a "shower."
6. At the wedding, the guests give the couple money or gifts.
7. People send the family condolence cards.
8. Some people send charities contributions.
9. Some people send the family flowers.

Exercise 4

Sentences will vary according to the students in the class. Students can also work in a group here and list the customs from their countries to be shared later with the whole class. You might put newsprint paper up in different parts of the room where students could write their sentences about birth customs, marriage customs, etc.

Focus 3

This Focus Box presents another instance of the discourse rule governing the position of given and new information in English. Both of the sentences presented here are grammatically correct, but there is an important difference when the sentences are used in context. The answer to the question, "Whom did you give a present to?" would more naturally be, "I gave a present **to my coworker**" and not "I gave my coworker a present." The two exercises that follow this Use Box provide specific contexts in which learners need to make discourse choices.

Exercise 5

1. I gave a present to my coworker.
   OR
   I gave it to my coworker.

2. I gave my parents tickets to a play.
   OR
   I gave them tickets to a play.

3. I told the joke to my friend.
   OR
   I told it to my friend.

4. I sent her some new recipes.

5. I lent the money to Pam.
   OR
   I lent it to Pam.

6. I read the children "Cinderella."
   OR
   I read them "Cinderella."

7. I mailed the application to the admissions office.
   OR
   I mailed it to the admissions office.

Exercise 6

1. (a)
2. (b)
3. (a)
4. (a)
5. (a)
6. (b)
7. (a)
8. (a)

Exercise 7

(1) I gave her✗ (a pair of diamond earrings).

(2) I gave (the scarf)✗ to my uncle.

(3) I gave my dad✗ (a set of golf clubs).

(4) I sent him✗ (some mystery novels and a subscription to *Money Magazine*).

(5) I wrote him✗ (a long letter).

(6) Oh, my bank sent me✗ (a huge credit card bill)!

Exercise 8

1. I gave him golf clubs.
2. Paul wrote her a letter.
3. The salesman sold them a bad car.
4. We owed him money.
5. The department store sent <u>us</u> the wrong stereo. [Note that "<u>my husband and me</u>" should be underlined in the students' book.]
6. The postman handed him a package.
7. The teacher read them the story.
8. I told her the problem.
9. Karen mailed it to the bank.
10. Our children wrote us a beautiful letter.

Exercise 9

1. Pattern A and Pattern B are possible.
2. Pattern A and Pattern B are possible.
3. Circle Pattern B. Only Pattern A is possible.
4. Circle Pattern B. Only Pattern A is possible.
5. Circle Pattern B. Only Pattern A is possible.
6. Pattern A and Pattern B are possible.
7. Pattern A and Pattern B are possible.
8. Circle Pattern B. Only Pattern A is possible.
9. Pattern A and Pattern B are possible.
10. Circle Pattern B. Only Pattern A is possible.

Activities

Activity 1

This is a fun game that engages students in meaningful communication. You might want students to create larger game boards with oak tag on which they could paste pictures of different "gifts" cut out from magazines. Students need a pair of dice and markers (coins, paper clips, markers from other games) so they can land on the boxes. A lot of authentic language comes out of this activity. You may want to walk around as students are playing and take notes on mistakes they make, which you will work on later. You may also want to give students some "game language" before playing — e.g., "It's your turn," "Time's up," etc.

Activity 2

As students are doing this activity, tape-record them so that they can transcribe the tape and look at the language they used. You might also want to focus on those squares that were problematic and elicit the correct language as a follow-up. In this way, students would be evaluating themselves, and saying which squares they had difficulty with and need practice on.

Activity 3

You or the students will probably need to make a bigger chart to record the answers.

Reflexive and Reciprocal Pronouns

Task

To set this task in motion, bring in some real advice columns such as "Dear Abby" from the newspaper to give students an understanding of the context.

Part B: Letters of Advice

- **A.** Dear Guilty,
- **B.** Dear Crazy Man,
- **C.** Dear Supermom,
- **D.** Dear Overweight,

Exercise 1

1. Don't blame (yourself). You did not cause the problems. This is your parents' problem.

2. Explain how you feel to her. Tell her you want to go out once a month. Tell her life is too short. Go out and enjoy (yourselves)!

3. You need to do something special for (yourself). Go out with your friends once in a while. Buy (yourself) a new dress.

4. Follow your doctor's advice. Take care of (yourself). Go on a diet. You're only hurting (yourself) when you smoke, so quit!

Exercise 2

1. (a) myself
   (b) yourself
2. (a) ourselves
   (b) themselves
3. (a) yourselves
4. (a) himself

Focus 2

In English, when we talk about routine actions that people obviously do themselves (dress, shave, wash), we do not use the reflexive pronoun. It might be helpful to point out that in some languages (French and Spanish, for example), the reflexive pronoun **is** used in these cases.

Exercise 3

Possible answers:

1. The man is shaving in the bathroom.
2. The man is looking at himself in the mirror.
3. The woman cut herself.
4. The woman is drying herself.
5. People are enjoying themselves at a party.
6. The child fell off the bicycle and hurt himself.
7. The old man is sitting on a park bench and talking to himself.
8. The cat is cleaning itself.

Exercise 4

Have students compare their drawings.

Picture (a)

Picture (b)

DUANE GILLOGLY

Exercise 5

Students act out the sentences. Another way of doing this exercise is to have pairs of students perform in front of the class. The class then makes statements about what they are doing.

Exercise 6

This exercise gives students practice in all types of pronouns — subject and object pronouns and reflexives. It also reviews possessive pronouns as well as possessive adjectives.

```
Dear Betty:
```

(My) boyfriend is very vain. (He) is very proud of (himself). He always looks at (himself) in store windows when he passes by. (He) only thinks about (himself). He never brings (me) flowers. The last time he told (me) that he loved me was two years ago. He never lends me (his) car. He says that the car is (his) and he doesn't want me to use it. Do (you) have any suggestions?

"Frustrated"

```
Dear "Frustrated":
```

(Your) boyfriend is very self-centered. (You) can't really change (him). Get rid of (him)! Find (yourself) a new guy!

Betty

97

Exercise 7

1. I hurt myself.
2. They're looking at themselves in the mirror.
3. I shave every morning.
4. We write to each other every month.
5. We enjoyed ourselves at the circus.
6. They blamed each other for the accident.
7. He did it himself.

Activities

Activity 1

This is based on a well-known logic problem that some students may be familiar with. Have students work in groups so they can try to figure it out together. Make sure students don't look at the answer at the bottom of the page. You could pose certain questions to guide them (e.g., *Why do you think there is a puddle? How could the puddle have formed? Do you think somebody else murdered the prisoner?*).

Activity 2

When students identify the most independent people in class, ask them to justify their decisions.

Activity 3

Students might need some time to work on this activity individually in order to reflect on their personal answers. They then could be put in pairs to discuss their answers.

UNIT 23

Future Time
Will and Be Going To

Task

Before starting this task, you might want to talk about predictions, fortune-tellers, etc., and probe students' experiences with the subject. In addition, you also may want to have students identify the people in the task (i.e., the fortune-teller, the female executive/businesswoman, the handsome man/bachelor, the elderly couple, the overweight man, the scientist, the rock star, the director, the lifeguard, the young couple, the poor/homeless man, the bald man, the king).

1. E.
2. J.
3. B.
4. K.
5. A.
6. H.
7. L.
8. I.
9. G.
10. C.
11. D.
12. F.

Focus 1

This Focus Box deals with the function **predicting,** which *will* and *going to* have in common, while trying to explain the difference in meaning between *will,* which is more hypothetical and more abstract, and *going to,* which is more grounded in a present reality.

Focus 2

The form of the modal *will* is introduced here, and in the exercises that follow, students practice using *will.*

Exercise 1

1. The executive will get a raise at work.
2. The young bachelor will meet a tall, dark, beautiful stranger.
3. The old couple will have ten grandchildren.
4. The overweight man will lose fifty pounds in two weeks.
5. The young boy will become a rock star.
6. The film director will produce a new movie and get rich.

7. The lifeguard will rescue someone and win a medal.
8. The young couple will get married.
9. The poor person will find $1,000 on the street.
10. The bald man will grow hair on his head.
11. The king will stay in power for fifty more years.

Exercise 2

Answers will depend on the students' personal views of the future. Interesting discussions should ensue. Possible answers include:

1. The weather will get warmer.
2. Pollution will get worse.
3. Staying in the sun will be more dangerous.
4. Poor people won't become richer.
5. All countries won't share the world's wealth equally.
6. People won't need money.
7. The traditional family will disappear.
8. People of different races will learn to love each other.
9. Women will earn more money than men.
10. People will work only four days a week.
11. Scientists will discover a cure for AIDS.
12. Cars will run on solar power.
13. People will live to be 110 years old.
14. We will communicate with beings on other planets.
15. We will not [or won't] produce weapons.
16. We will not [or won't] fight wars.
17. A woman will become Prime Minister of Canada.
18. We will have three political parties in the United States.

Exercise 3

Students make true statements about themselves.

Exercise 4

1. Will my husband lose his job?
2. Will my husband/he find another job?
3. When will my husband/he find another job?
4. Will my daughter get married?
5. Who(m) will she marry?
6. Will I have grandchildren?
7. How many grandchildren will I have?
8. Will my son go to college?

9. What will he do?
10. Will my husband and I retire?
11. Where will we retire?

Exercise 5

This exercise encourages students to discuss their answers using *there will be* or *there won't be,* e.g.:

There won't be any crime. There will be poverty.

Focus 3

The form of *be going to* is presented in this Box and practiced in the exercises that follow.

Exercise 6

1. Watch out! You're going to hit him!
2. Hurry up! We're going to miss the bus.
3. This isn't going to hurt you one bit.
4. I am exhausted! I'm going to take a nap.
5. They're going to have a baby.
6. **George:** OK. I'm going to have just one more doughnut.
   Woman: That's what you always say, George. You aren't going to lose weight this way!
7. Watch her, Jack! She's going to fall into the pool!
8. **Husband:** Good night, honey. I'm going to go to bed.
   Wife: OK, Matt. I'm going to watch the news for a while.

Exercise 7

Answers will vary.

Exercise 8

1. Where are you going to go?
2. When are you going to go? / to leave?
3. What time are you going to go there? / to leave?
4. How are you going to go? / to get there?
5. Who(m) are you going to go with?
6. What are you going to do at the beach?
7. How much money are you going to bring? / to spend? / to take?
8. Are you going to have a good time? / to have fun?

Exercise 9

Students are free to invent answers using *going to*. This exercise may be done orally or in writing. Some examples:
1. He's going to buy some new clothes.
2. He's going to meet her at a party.

Exercise 10

1. (a) at   (b) on
2. for
3. on
4. until
5. in
6. until
7. At
8. for
9. on

Exercise 11

1. at 6:00
2. next week / next Friday / on April 19 / on Friday the 19th
3. tomorrow / on Thursday / on April 11
4. the day after tomorrow / on Friday / on April 12
5. next week / next Thursday / a week from Thursday
6. next week / next Tuesday / on April 16
7. next month / on May 6 / in five weeks
8. on June 10 / in two months
9. in 1999 / in _____ years
10. in 2005 / in _____ years

Focus 6

This Focus Box differentiates between *will*, used when the speaker decides to do something at the time of speaking, and *going to*, used to express future actions that have already been planned, or arranged at the time of speaking.

Exercise 12

This exercise gets students to practice the distinction between *will* and *be going to*, and is obviously more challenging.

1. A.
2. B.
3. B.
4. A.
5. A.
6. B.
7. A.
8. A.
9. A.
10. B.

Activities

Activity 1

Create an atmosphere of a New Year's Eve party. Have everyone make toasts (with ginger ale, of course!) and state their resolutions aloud. You may want to ask if people in other cultures also make New Year's resolutions.

Activity 2

Have the groups write their predictions on newsprint, post them in front of the room, and discuss them. Decide who the optimists in the class are, and who the pessimists are.

Activity 3

This is a very good activity to do after students have known each other a while. You can encourage students to be creative and use their imagination. It might be helpful to choose a "good sport" in the class and have students generate different predictions for that student to give everyone an idea of the possibilities. At the end of the activity, students retain their original papers with all the predictions of the students in the class.

Activity 5

Make sure that students get as specific as possible. Bring pictures to class to give students ideas of the variety of things they can do. You could even have students illustrate their plans.

UNIT 24

Quantifiers

Task

You will need to spend some time discussing the concepts of calories, fat, and cholesterol in foods. Bring in pictures showing foods high in calories, fat, and cholesterol, and foods that are not, to get the meaning across.

1. 3
2. 1 glass
3. 3
4. 21 milligrams
5. none/0
6. the vanilla milkshake
7. 4.6 grams
8. Bobby's: 375
   Billy's: 655
   Brad's: 940
9. 486 milligrams in Billy's
   0 milligrams in Bobby's
   49 milligrams in Brad's
10. a muffin
11. eggs, sausages, whole milk
12. cereal, orange juice, skim milk, bananas
13. Bobby

Focus 1

Before doing this Focus Box, you may want to review count/non-count nouns by eliciting from students what they remember from Unit 4.

Exercise 1

Count Nouns:

eggs	pancakes
sausages	doughnuts
muffin	vanilla milkshake
bananas	

Non-Count Nouns:

milk
cereal
juice

Exercise 2

This exercise demonstrates the relative nature of quantifiers, where meaning depends on the speaker. For example, in this exercise we are saying that the answer to "Carlos has a lot of money in the bank" is letter "D." Some students might argue that "C" is also possible if they think that $500 is a lot of money. These answers can be discussed.

<u> D. </u> 1. (For some students, "C" might mean "a lot of money.")
<u> B. </u> 2. (For some students, "C" might mean "a little money.")
<u> A. </u> 3.
<u> C. </u> 4. (For some students, "B" might mean "some money.")
<u> E. </u> 5.
<u> G. </u> 6.
<u> F. </u> 7.

Exercise 3

Students draw pictures to represent each statement. Since the meaning of a quantifier is relative, it would be a good idea to look at the three pictures the students draw to see what "a lot of" vs. "a few" is, etc.

Exercise 4

Incorrect Quantifiers:

1. a few
2. many
3. a little
4. much
5. many

Exercise 5

Answers may vary. You can collect all the statements that students generate and put them together to form a review quiz.

Exercise 6

This is an *Information Gap Exercise,* so be sure that one student is looking at the incomplete recipes and covering up the answers found in the complete recipes below. The questions students must ask are the following:

> 1. How many potatoes do I need?
>   How much bacon…
>   How many onions…
>   How much vinegar…
>   How much olive oil…
>   How much salt and pepper…
>   How much parsley…

2. How many tomatoes do I need? How much tomato juice…
How many red peppers…   How many eggs…
How many onions…   How much cayenne pepper…
How many cucumbers…   How much salt and pepper…
How much vinegar…   How much dill…
How much olive oil…

Exercise 7

1. (a) few   (b) little
2. a few
3. little
4. little
5. (a) a few   (b) a little

Exercise 8

a pound of	coffee	**a quart/gallon of**	oil
a quart/a half-gallon of	milk	**a bottle of**	soda
a bag of	rice	**2 loaves of**	bread
two cans of	soup	**3 bars of**	soap
a tube of	toothpaste	**a head of**	lettuce
a bag of	candy	**2 rolls of**	toilet paper
3 bottles of	beer	**a pound of**	beef
a half-pound of	butter	**a jar of**	peanut butter

Exercise 9

1. Jane: Can I talk to you for a minute?
   Kevin: Sure, I have a little time.
2. John has many friends/a lot of friends.
3. How much money do you have?
4. My teacher gave us a lot of homework.
5. My hair is black.
6. She jogs a few miles a day.
7. We don't sell any newspapers here.
8. There are many opportunities/a lot of opportunities in this city.
9. I would like some information please.
10. My friend gave me some/a lot of advice.

Activities

Activity 1

If students have questions about the validity of these statements, have them go to the library and do some research. Or bring in health or consumer magazines in which they might find these facts.

Activity 2

After doing this activity, students can decide who has the healthiest diet in the group. This activity should provoke a lot of discussion.

Activity 3

If you have a very large class, this might be tedious and take too long. You could break the class up into two groups and have two circles going on simultaneously. The game tends to be a lot of fun, and students are challenged with having to remember all the information.

Activity 4

Bring in a variety of menus for students to practice with. Have students tape-record their orders. Their simulations can be played back or transcribed and analyzed for grammar mistakes.

Activity 5

You might want to have students volunteer to present a recipe to the class.

Adjective Phrases

Task

This is a complex two-step task where students must match a person to each statement, as well as match all the people to the houses they live in. Have students work in pairs to figure this out and then have two pairs work together to check their answers.

Part A

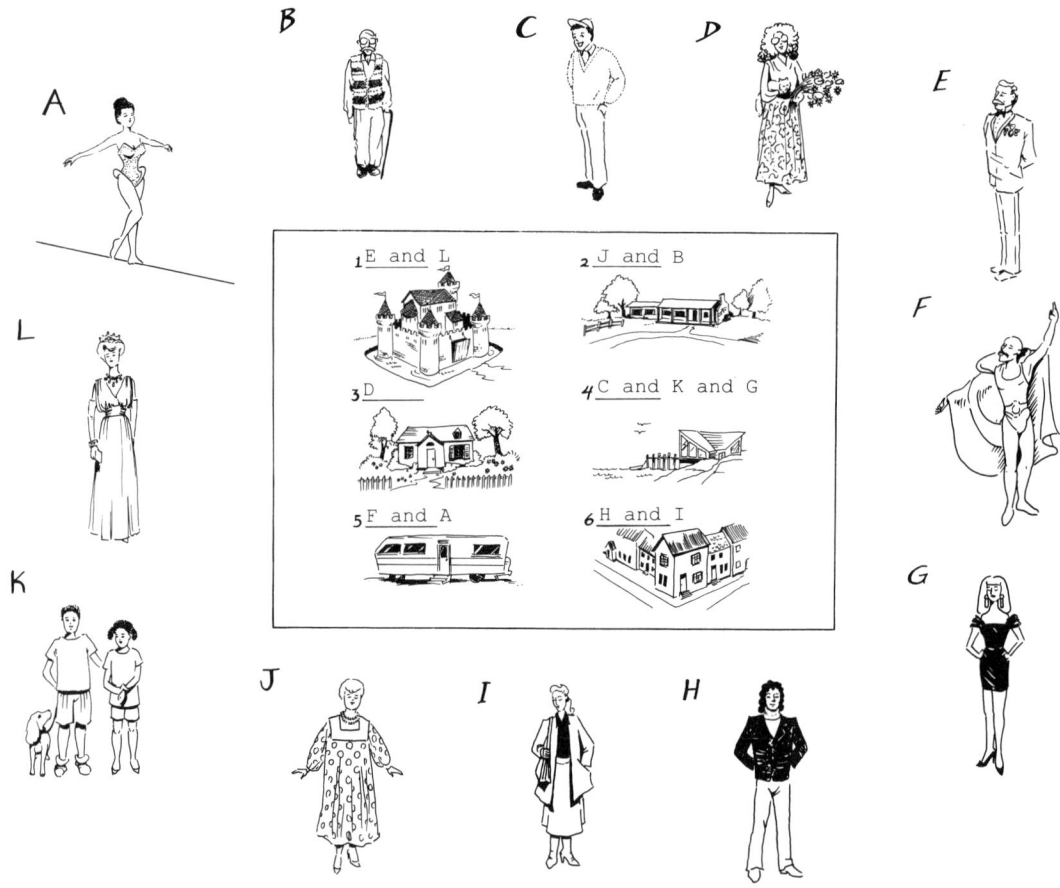

Part B

1. F
2. E
3. H
4. D
5. L
6. J
7. B
8. K
9. C
10. I
11. A
12. G

Exercise 1

1. The bald man (with a mustache) has an athletic wife.
2. The man (with the medals on his jacket) lives in house #1.
3. The man (in the dark jacket and turtle-neck sweater) is an accountant and lives in house #6.
4. The woman (with the flowers) is the occupant of house #3.
5. The retired woman (with the crown on her head) is married to the man in house #1.
6. The woman (in the polka-dot dress) lives in house #2.
7. The man (in the striped vest) is married to the retired woman.
8. The children (with the dog) live with their parents.
9. The man (with the cap) lives in house #4.
10. The woman (with the bag over her shoulder) is married to the accountant.
11. The woman (on the tightrope) lives in house #5.
12. The woman (in the high heel shoes) has two children.

Focus 2

The difficulty in forming adjective phrases is in knowing which phrase is embedded in which, and which preposition is to be used in combining the two sentences. We have indicated different examples here to illustrate this. Note that **(e)** and **(f)** are different from **(a)** through **(d)**. The last two examples, **(g)** and **(h)**, simply use the same preposition of location.

Exercise 2

Have students try to identify where they would usually find these chairs before doing the exercise since this general knowledge may be culturally bound.

#	Chair	Answer	Sentence
1.	A	7	The man with the crown sits in chair A.
2.	B	1	The man with the megaphone sits in chair B.
3.	C	3	The girl with the popcorn sits in chair C.
4.	D	4	The woman with the mirror sits in chair D.
5.	E	10	The man with the whistle sits in chair E.
6.	F	8	The boy with the books sits in chair F.
7.	G	2	The baby with the bottle sits in chair G.
8.	H	5	The man with the suitcases sits in chair H.
9.	I	6	The woman with the cane sits in chair I.
10.	J	9	The girl with the ice cream cone sits in chair J.

Exercise 3

1. The girl with the pigtails is kicking her partner.
2. The boy in/with the baseball cap is throwing a paper airplane across the room.
3. The girls near the window are waving to friends outside.
4. The boy in the Ninja Turtle suit is standing on the teacher's desk.
5. The boys in the back of the room are fighting.
6. The boy in the corner is reading.
7. The girl in the closet is crying.
8. The girl with the walkman is singing.
9. The man with a rope around him is the new teacher.
10. The man in the suit and tie is the principal.
11. The new teacher in this story will lose his job.

Exercise 4

Have students identify the rooms in the house first. Starting on the first floor on the left, there is the living room, then the dining room, and next to the dining room is the kitchen. Upstairs on the left is the bedroom, then the den, and the bathroom.

1. **Student A:** The window is broken.
   Student B: Which window is broken?
   Student A: The one in the kitchen.

2. **Student A:** The curtains are torn.
   Student B: Which curtains are torn?
   Student A: The ones in the living room.

3. **Student A:** The TV is missing.
   Student B: Which TV is missing?
   Student A: The one in the den/room upstairs.

4. **Student A:** The door is open.
   Student B: Which door is open?
   Student A: The one in/to the kitchen.

5. **Student A:** The lamp is broken.
   Student B: Which lamp is broken?
   Student A: The one in the den/room upstairs.

6. **Student A:** The VCR is missing.
   Student B: Which VCR is missing?
   Student A: The one in the living room.

7. **Student A:** The lock is broken.
   Student B: Which lock is broken?
   Student A: The one on the kitchen door.

8. **Student A:** The rug is missing.
   Student B: Which rug is missing?
   Student A: The one in the bedroom.

Activities

Activity 2

Have students mount their photographs on poster board and write their descriptions under them for all students to read.

Activity 3

Have each student write his or her sentences on newsprint in the front of the room. Errors can be corrected. This could also be turned into an activity in which students are promoting the countries or cities they come from. They could do short presentations, advertising their countries for travel purposes.

Phrasal Verbs

Task

To facilitate this task, you might have students make up cards like the ones in the task (i.e., have them write each direction on separate index cards). Students put the cards in order, and then one set of students could post their cards on the board so everyone could check their order. Note that some variation is possible.

- Stand up and walk to the table at the front of the room.
- Take out my notes.
- Turn on the slide projector.
- Turn off the lights.
- Show the slides.
- Turn off the projector.
- Ask for questions.
- Hand out the evaluation forms.
- Go back to my seat.
- Sit down.

Exercise 1

(Stand up) and walk to the table at the front of the room.

(Take out) my notes.

(Turn on) the slide projector.

(Turn off) the lights.

Show the slides.

(Turn off) the projector.

Ask for questions.

(Hand out) the evaluation forms.

(Go back) to my seat.

(Sit down).

Focus 2

Phrasal verbs present many problems for ESL students. They should be encouraged to try to understand phrasal verbs in context and to use them actively, not simply look up their meanings in the dictionary.

Exercise 2

1. Enter
2. Relax
3. Extinguish
4. Distribute
5. Telephone
6. Return
7. Lower
8. Raise
9. Remove
10. Discard

Exercise 3

1. Turn the projector on.
   Turn it on.
2. Turn the lights off.
   Turn them off.
3. Hand the evaluations out.
   Hand them out.
4. Take your jackets off.
   Take them off.
5. Throw your gum away.
   Throw it away.
6. Look your notes over.
   Look them over.
7. Put your cigarettes out.
   Put them out.

Exercise 4

(1) pick up   (2) turn off   (3) pull out   (4) put away   (5) throw away   (6) turn on

Exercise 5

1. Let's eat out.
2. Take off your sweater.
3. Turn on the radio.
4. Put on your glasses.
5. Turn off the TV.
6. Get up early.
7. Sit down and rest.
8. Slow down.
9. Calm down.
10. Stand up for a few minutes.

Exercise 6

(1) figure out   (2) call up   (3) picked up   (4) went over   (5) hang up

Exercise 7

1. (a) fill   (b) out
   (c) fill   (d) it   (e) out
2. (a) take   (b) out
   (c) taking   (d) it   (e) out
3. (a) pick   (b) up
   (c) pick   (d) it   (e) up
4. (a) hand   (b) out
   (c) hand   (d) them   (e) out

Exercise 8

1. A: Did you pick up our clothes at the cleaners?
   B: Yes, I picked them up.

2. A: Did you hang up the clean clothes?
   B: Yes, I hung them up.

3. A: Did you put away the clean laundry?
   B: Yes, I put it away.

4. A: Did you take out the dog?
   B: Yes, I took him out.

5. A: Did you throw out the garbage?
   B: Yes, I threw it out.

6. A: Did you pick up something for dinner?
   B: Yes, I picked it up./I picked something up.

7. A: Did you put up dinner?
   B: Yes, I put it up.

8. A: Did you turn on the movie for the children?
   B: Yes, I turned it on.

9. A: Did you call up your mother?
   B: Yes, I called her up.

10. A: Did you clean up the kitchen?
    B: Yes, I cleaned it up.

Activities

Activity 1

Give each pair or group a large sheet of newsprint and felt-tip pens. Each pair can write and display their story. Students can circulate to compare their stories with those of their classmates. For additional practice, bring in other pictures, cartoons, or illustrations and provide students with phrasal verbs to write a story or dialogue.

Activity 2

To vary this activity, give each group a different context in which to create their dialogue. For example, one group could be good friends with their neighbors, whereas another group could have a longstanding problem with the neighbors.

Activity 3

As a follow-up to this activity, have students create their own phrasal verb grid.

UNIT 27

Comparison with Adjectives

Task

Discuss the information about the cars so students are familiar with the vocabulary required to do the task.

1. F
2. T
3. T
4. T
5. F
6. F
7. T
8. F
9. F
10. Students write their own opinion.

Exercise 1

This exercise heightens students' awareness of the rules for forming the comparative.

Comparative	Rule
1. longer than	3.
2. bigger than	2.
3. wider than	1.
4. safer than	1.
5. more powerful than	5.
6. more economical than	5.
7. more expensive than	5.
8. heavier than	4.
9. more comfortable than	5.
10. prettier than	4.

Exercise 2

	Adjective	# of Syllables	Comparative Form
1.	large	1	*larger than*
2.	enthusiastic	5	*more enthusiastic than*
3.	busy	2	*busier than*
4.	exciting	3	*more exciting than*
5.	intelligent	4	*more intelligent than*
6.	hot	1	*hotter than*
7.	nervous	2	*more nervous than*
8.	comfortable	4 (*or* 3)	*more comfortable than*
9.	crazy	2	*crazier than*
10.	sad	1	*sadder than*

Exercise 3

To make this exercise more interesting and engaging, you might have students present advertisements and then decide which presentation was the most convincing. Give students additional vocabulary if necessary.

Answers may vary. Possible answers include:

1. Sinful Delight is { richer than / creamier than / more delicious than / moister than / sweeter than / thicker than / less fattening than } Choco-Bake.

2. Suds Plus is { stronger than / more effective than / more expensive than / quicker than } Bubbles Soap.

3. Save-a-Watt Space Heater is { more efficient than / safer than / more reliable than / bigger than / easier (to use) than / more economical than / more practical than } Consumer Space Heater.

Exercise 4

Answers may vary. Possible answers include:

2. Los Angeles is more populated than Brattleboro.
   Brattleboro is less populated than Los Angeles.

3. A one-bedroom apartment in Brattleboro is cheaper than a one-bedroom apartment in Los Angeles.
   An apartment in Los Angeles is more expensive than an apartment in Brattleboro.

4. Public transportation in Brattleboro is worse than in Los Angeles.
   Public transportation in Los Angeles is better than in Brattleboro.

5. Winters are colder in Brattleboro than in Los Angeles.
   Summers are hotter in Los Angeles than in Brattleboro.

6. It's more dangerous in Los Angeles than in Brattleboro.
   Brattleboro is safer than Los Angeles.

7. Brattleboro is cleaner than Los Angeles.
   Los Angeles is dirtier than Brattleboro.

Exercise 5

Students generate yes/no questions from the Task.

Exercise 6

Some of these examples could provoke interesting discussion. You might want to open up the discussion to the whole class, in particular, Examples 2, 5, and 9.

1. Is a theater ticket more expensive than a movie ticket?
2. Are people in the United States friendlier than people in your native country?
3. Is English grammar more difficult than the grammar of your language?
4. Is an IBM computer easier to use than a Macintosh™ computer?
5. Is reading more interesting than watching TV?
6. Is fried chicken more fattening than broiled chicken?
7. Is fast food better than a homemade meal?
8. Is electric heat more economical than gas heat?
9. Are men more emotional than women?
10. Is a Japanese watch more expensive than a Swiss watch?

Exercise 7

The examples in this exercise are more subjective and generate more discussion. Have students choose the questions they might like to discuss at greater length.

1. Who is more intelligent, men or women?
2. Which is more difficult, speaking English or writing English?

3. Which is worse, ironing or vacuuming?
4. Which is cheaper, a city college or a private college?
5. Which is more powerful, a 4-cylinder car or a 5-cylinder car?
6. Which is more dangerous, a motorcycle or a car?
7. Who is more sensitive, women or men?
8. Which is more delicious, Chinese food or Italian food?
9. Which is spicier, Indian food or Thai food?
10. Which is more useful, a typewriter or a computer?
11. Which is heavier, a ton of feathers or a ton of bricks?
    (**Answer:** Neither — they both weigh the same!)

Exercise 8

(1) more convenient than
(2) more practical
(3) as economical as
(4) cheaper than
(5) safer than
(6) better than/as good as
(7) more aware of
(8) easier
(9) older

Exercise 9

1. London is not as clean as Paris.
2. Science class isn't as interesting as math class.
3. Your child isn't as intelligent as mine.
4. This book is not as good as that book.
5. Your apartment is not as large as ours.
6. Miguel's pronunciation is not as good as Maria's.
7. American coffee isn't as strong as Turkish coffee.

Exercise 10

Student-generated exercise. Answers will vary.

Exercise 11

1. John is taller than Mary.
2. Tokyo is safer than New York City.
3. Paul is as selfish as Robert/more selfish than Robert.
4. Mary is not as beautiful as Kim.
5. My test scores were worse than Margaret's.

Activities

Activity 1

A chart would facilitate these comparisons:

Country	Cost of...				
	Gallon of Gas	Movie Ticket	Bus Fare	Pair of Jeans	Cup of Coffee

You could also create one large class chart and list all the countries. As a homework assignment, students could write comparative statements, using the information in the chart.

Activity 3

This activity will encourage students to discuss their personalities in order to determine how talkative, extroverted, shy, etc., they are. You might need to review some of the adjectives with them first.

Activity 4

As a follow-up to this activity, bring in apartment ads from the classifieds and have students compare and choose apartments.

Activity 5

Put on a class advertising campaign. Encourage the pairs to come up with creative and interesting products and present their products in front of the class. Decide which ad was the most convincing, the funniest, the most original, etc.

Activity 6

Have students share their writings.

UNIT 28
Comparison with Adverbs

Task

Students should first work on this task individually, taking some time to think about their own personal opinions on these questions. Obviously there are no correct answers to these questions, but they will provoke discussion.

Exercise 1

1. Do women live <u>longer than</u> men?
2. Do men drive <u>more safely than</u> women?
3. Do women communicate <u>better than</u> men?
4. Do women manage people <u>better than</u> men do?
5. Do men work <u>harder than</u> women?
6. Do women dance <u>more gracefully than</u> men do?
7. Do men think <u>more clearly than</u> women do in emergencies?
8. Do women take care of children <u>more patiently than</u> men?
9. Do women express their feelings <u>more openly than</u> men do?
10. Can women learn languages <u>more easily than</u> men?
11. Can men do math <u>more easily than</u> women?
12. Do women spend money <u>more freely than</u> men?

Exercise 2

Students generate their own responses using the comparative form of adverbs. Answers will vary.

Exercise 3

Answers may vary. Possible answers include:

3. Sally thinks as creatively as Bill (does).
4. Sally communicates more openly than Bill (does).
5. Sally treats workers more fairly than Bill (does).
6. Sally reacts to problems more calmly than Bill (does).
7. Bill prepares more diligently than Sally does.
8. Bill thinks through problems more carefully than Sally (does).
9. Sally writes as clearly as Bill (does).
10. Bill works faster than Sally (does).

Exercise 4

Students generate their own questions about Sally and Bill. Possible questions:

1. Does Sally work as hard as Bill?
2. Does Bill draw more artistically than Sally?
3. Does Bill think as creatively as Sally?
4. Does Sally communicate more openly than Bill?

Exercise 5

Students generate their own sentences here. Emphasis should be placed on intonation, especially if students are disagreeing with the statements made.

Exercise 6

Discussion of the prereading questions will provide students with some background knowledge of this topic. This knowledge, introduced along with relevant vocabulary, will also make the reading easier and more accessible to the students. You might try interrupting the reading after the first paragraph and having students predict what differences will be described. Again, eliciting predictions, hypotheses, and vocabulary from the students first will enhance their reading ability. Ask learners to guess the meanings of certain words (*boast, argue, intimacy*) in context.

Exercise 7

1. True
2. True/False. *Answers may vary because girls and boys are social in different ways!*
3. False
4. False
5. True
6. True
7. True
8. False

Exercise 8

Answers will vary according to the sex and views of the learner. Some examples:

1. Girls score higher on math tests.
2. Boys run faster than girls.

Exercise 9

1. How long does it take you to get dressed in the morning?
2. How far do you live from school?
3. How long does it take you to get to school?
4. How well do you cook?

5. How fast do you drive?
6. How far can/do you run?
7. How hard do you study?
8. How long does it take you to clean your apartment/house?

Exercise 10

Answers will vary.

Activities

Activity 2

This is a fun activity that could be used as a review or a way of making sure that students understand how to use adverbs of comparison. To vary this activity, have students generate a new list of adverbs and actions, or use pictures or videos to elicit comparisons with adverbs.

Activity 3

As students are working in groups to plan out their itinerary, encourage them to use questions with "how far" and "how long." You may also ask these questions to make sure that they understand. You can have groups present their itineraries and then have the class ask more specific questions about distance and time to practice the forms.

Superlatives

Task

Have students work in groups of four to five, thereby increasing the chances that other students might know some of the answers to these trivia questions.

1. The Great Wall of China
2. The common cold
3. The *Mona Lisa* by Leonardo da Vinci (1452–1519) in the Louvre, Paris
4. Northern Chinese or Mandarin
5. Dallol, Ethiopia, with an average annual temperature of 94 degrees Fahrenheit.
6. The Sears Tower in Chicago with 110 stories.
7. Mexico City
8. *Gone With the Wind* with Clark Gable and Vivien Leigh was released in 1939 and is the highest in box office gross. *E.T.* is the second most popular film.
9. M.I.T. (Massachusetts Institute of Technology)
10. Diamond, which is chemically pure carbon, is the hardest gem.

Focus 2

Check that students understand the difference between *farther* (physical distance) and *further* (both physical and metaphysical distance).

Exercise 1

1. the longest
2. the most common
3. the most valuable
4. the most common
5. the hottest
6. the tallest
7. the biggest
8. the most popular
9. the most expensive
10. the hardest

Exercise 2

Some of the vocabulary might initially be difficult for students. Encourage them to guess the meanings of new words in context (e.g., *prolific*), or explain the vocabulary. The facts are surprising and interesting to students.

1. The largest
2. The most popular
3. The most successful
4. The heaviest
5. The fattest
6. The most prolific
7. The longest
8. The biggest

Exercise 3

Students write their own answers in the blanks.

1. _____ is one of the most beautiful cities in the world.
2. _____ is one of the most interesting places in this city.
3. _____ is one of the best restaurants in this city.
4. _____ is one of the most dangerous diseases in the world.
5. _____ is one of the most serious problems in the world.
6. _____ is one of the worst movies.
7. _____ is one of the most popular foods in _____.
8. _____ is one of the greatest books of all time.

Exercise 4

This exercise is based on the television game show Jeopardy™. Since students work in groups, they can rely on each other's background knowledge to find the question for the answer given. In addition, all groups are encouraged to work simultaneously to find the question so that students are not sitting idly and losing interest.

	Planets	Animals	Other
$10	Jupiter	giraffe	Tokyo
$20	Mercury	mosquitoes	The Sahara
$30	Venus	cheetah	June 21
$40	Pluto	thoroughbred race horses (cash value)	December 21
$50	Venus	blue or sulfur-bottom whale	The Supreme Court

Exercise 5

Information Gap Exercise. Answers are provided in the exercise. Questions include:

What's the longest river in _____?

What's the largest country in _____?

What's the most populous country in _____?

What's the highest mountain in _____?

What's the smallest country in _____?

Activities

Activity 1

After students write their questions, you can have each group ask another group their questions. If the group gets the answer, they get five points.

Activity 2

Have students write their questions on butcher block paper so that you can do error correction before they do their interviews.

Activity 3

This discussion can also lead into a writing activity which you can collect and check. You could also expand this activity to stereotypes if you feel that your class is prepared to handle this. They would generate statements that the whole class could analyze and discuss. (For example, "American children are the most spoiled children in the world"; "American society is the most violent/liberal/democratic in the world.")

Activity 4

To add another twist to this activity, you can have students work in groups, giving their answers to one of the questions. For example, students can talk about the most embarrassing moment in their life. The group can then choose the most interesting/most unusual/funniest embarrassing moment and act out or role-play the incident for the class.

UNIT 30: Factual Conditionals

Factual conditionals are rarely introduced in beginning level texts. They are dealt with here because, tense-wise, they are not difficult to manipulate. In addition, this unit provides the *if* clause/main clause structure needed for conditionals introduced later in the series.

Task

1. d.
2. i.
3. a.
4. f.
5. b.
6. h.
7. c.
8. j.
9. e.
10. g.

Exercise 1

Allow students time to figure out these problems in pairs or groups before discussing them as a class.

1. a.
2. a.
3. b.
4. a.
5. b.
6. b.
7. a.
8. a.
9. b.

Exercise 2

Possible answers:

1. you worry about them.
2. you share expenses.
3. you pay a lot of interest.
4. you feel great/rested/relaxed.
5. you use public transportation
6. you say "God bless you."

Exercise 3

Encourage students to discuss old wives' tales in their own culture. Have students write their tales on the blackboard or on butcher block paper so the class can read them.

Exercise 4

Have students figure out how long they will live, and then share their results with the class. You could ask them to suggest life-style changes that would guarantee a longer life!

Focus 4

The order of clauses in factual conditionals depends on the discourse rule governing given-new information. New information is postponed until the end of the sentences. Therefore, when the *if* clause contains the new information, it can occur in second position.

Exercise 5

Answers will vary. Possible answers include:

1. Milk turns sour if you don't refrigerate it.
2. I miss home whenever I don't receive any mail.
3. You catch a cold if you come into contact with a sick person.
4. I have trouble sleeping whenever I drink coffee at night.
5. My parents punished me whenever I did something wrong.
6. My parents were pleased with me whenever I got good grades.
7. I listen to music if I want to feel happy.
8. I get angry if I see injustice around me.
9. I learn English if I try to speak to Americans.
10. I reread this grammar book whenever I need to review something.

Activities

Activity 1

You might have to introduce the concepts of "Type A" and "Type B" people before having students proceed with the activity. Take a survey of how many "Type A" and "Type B" students there are in the class.

Activities 2 and 3

As a change of pace, have students record their sentences so that they can be played back to the whole class.

Activity 4

This activity will encourage students to share information about cultural habits. Have students work in groups to write their sentences. Then have the groups exchange their papers to compare them.